antietam 1862

the civil war's bloodiest day

NORMAN STEVENS

antietam 1862

the civil war's bloodiest day

Praeger Illustrated Military History Series

Westport, Connecticut
London

Library of Congress Cataloging-in-Publication Data

Stevens, Norman S.
   Antietam 1862: the Civil War's bloodiest day / Norman S. Stevens.
     p. cm. – (Praeger illustrated military history, ISSN 1547-206X)
   Originally published: Oxford: Osprey, 1994.
   Includes bibliographical references and index.
   ISBN 0-275-98442-7 (alk. paper)
   1. Antietam, Battle of, Md., 1862. I. Title. II. Series.
E474.65.S76   2004
973.7'336–dc22   2004049501

British Library Cataloguing in Publication Data is available.

First published in paperback in 1994 by Osprey Publishing Limited, Elms Court,
Chapel Way, Botley, Oxford OX2 9LP. All rights reserved.

Copyright © 2004 by Osprey Publishing Limited

Library of Congress Catalog Card Number: 2004049501
ISBN: 0-275-98442-7
ISSN: 1547-206X

Praeger Publishers, 88 Post Road West, Westport, CT 06881
An imprint of Greenwood Publishing Group, Inc.
www.praeger.com

Printed in China through World Print Ltd.

The paper used in this book complies with the Permanent Paper Standard issued
by the National Information Standards Organization (Z39.48-1984).

10 9 8 7 6 5 4 3 2 1

FRONT COVER: *'Burnside's Division at Antietam'*, Anne S. K. Brown Military Collection,
Brown University Library.

CONTENTS

The Campaign	**7**
McClellan Takes Command	7
Lee's Invasion of Maryland	9
Special Order 191	11
The Opposing Commanders	**15**
The Federal Commanders	15
The Confederate Commanders	17
The Opposing Armies	**21**
South Mountain	**33**
The Battle of Crampton's Gap	33
The Battle of Turner's Gap	35
Opposing Plans, 17 September 1862	**42**
Antietam: Hooker's Attack	**45**
I Corps Attacks	45
Hood's Counter-Attack	48
XII Corps Attacks	49
II Corps Attacks	53
The McLaws–Walker Couner-Attack	56
Antietam: Bloody Lane	**60**
The Initial Attacks	62
The Exposed Flank	64
Antietam: Burnside Bridge	**72**
The Crossing	75
The Attack on Sharpsburg	80
Hill to the Rescue	80
Aftermath	**85**
The Battlefield Today	**89**
Chronology	**91**
A Guide to Further Reading	**93**
Index	**95**

Key to Map Symbols

Army	XXXX ⊠	Brigade	X ⊠	Infantry	⊠
Corps	XXX ⊠	Regiment	III ⊠	Cavalry	◤
Division	XX ⊠	Battalion	II ⊠	Artillery	▫•

The Invasion of Maryland, September 1862

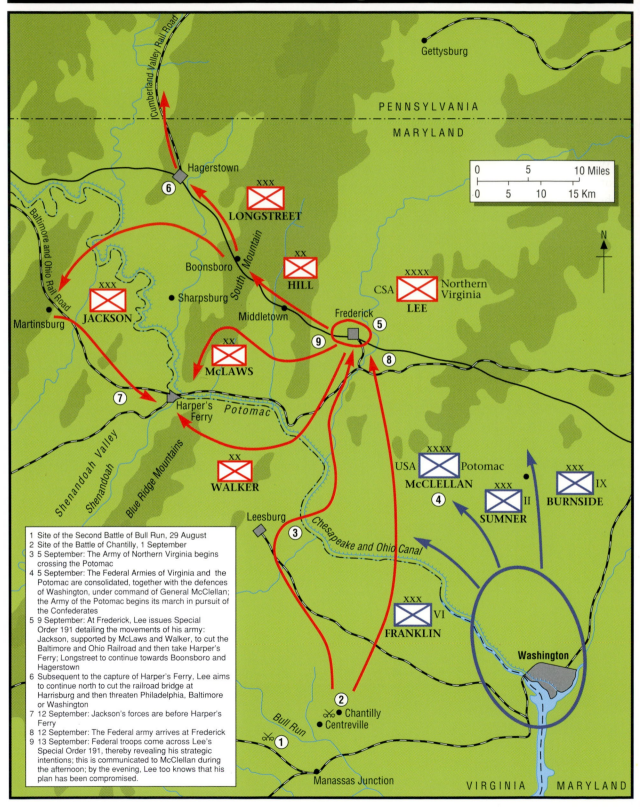

PENNSYLVANIA

MARYLAND

Gettysburg

Cumberland Valley Rail Road

Hagerstown

LONGSTREET xxx

6

Baltimore and Ohio Rail Road

Boonsboro

South Mountain

HILL xx

CSA

LEE xxxx Northern Virginia

JACKSON xxx

Sharpsburg

Martinsburg

Middletown

Frederick

5

9

McLAWS xx

8

Harper's Ferry

Potomac

7

Shenandoah Valley

Shenandoah

Blue Ridge Mountains

WALKER xx

USA

McCLELLAN xxxx Potomac

SUMNER xxx II

BURNSIDE xxx IX

4

Leesburg

3

Chesapeake and Ohio Canal

FRANKLIN xxx VI

Washington

0   5   10 Miles

0   5   10   15 Km

N

1 Site of the Second Battle of Bull Run, 29 August

2 Site of the Battle of Chantilly, 1 September

3 5 September: The Army of Northern Virginia begins crossing the Potomac

4 5 September: The Federal Armies of Virginia and the Potomac are consolidated, together with the defences of Washington, under command of General McClellan; the Army of the Potomac begins its march in pursuit of the Confederates

5 9 September: At Frederick, Lee issues Special Order 191 detailing the movements of his army: Jackson, supported by McLaws and Walker, to cut the Baltimore and Ohio Railroad and then take Harper's Ferry; Longstreet to continue towards Boonsboro and Hagerstown

6 Subsequent to the capture of Harper's Ferry, Lee aims to continue north to cut the railroad bridge at Harrisburg and then threaten Philadelphia, Baltimore or Washington

7 12 September: Jackson's forces are before Harper's Ferry

8 12 September: The Federal army arrives at Frederick

9 13 September: Federal troops come across Lee's Special Order 191, thereby revealing his strategic intentions; this is communicated to McClellan during the afternoon; by the evening, Lee too knows that his plan has been compromised.

Bull Run

Chantilly

Centreville

2

1

Manassas Junction

VIRGINIA   MARYLAND

THE CAMPAIGN

There was an unpleasant air of defeat hanging over the long, dusty blue columns of the Federal Army of Virginia as it sullenly retired on the Federal capital of Washington. At the two-day engagement of Second Manassas, fought near Centreville, Virginia, in the last days of August 1862, the Federal forces had been roughly handled. A determined rearguard action fought on 1 September by elements of the Federal IX Corps at Chantilly, or Ox Hill, led by Major General Isaac Ingalls Stevens prevented complete disaster; however, the retreat continued into the extensive fortifications of Washington. The Federal Army of Virginia had been thrown together hastily from various formations in the Shenandoah Valley and around Washington. The organization did not have time to sort itself out before it was engaged in a campaign with General Robert E. Lee's Confederate Army of Northern Virginia, fresh from driving Major General George McClellan's Federal Army of the Potomac away from Richmond. The individual soldier of the Federal Army of

Virginia believed that his regiment and his immediate comrades were capable of better effort than had been demonstrated at Second Manassas. The rank and file suspected that they had been forced to endure defective leadership. The men entertained no confidence in their army commander, Major General John Pope, nor in their corps leaders, Major Generals Franz Sigel, Nathaniel Banks, and Irwin McDowell. The Federal Army of Virginia was dispirited and acutely disappointed in their leadership as they approached the Federal Capital on the second day of September 1862. President Abraham Lincoln's summer gamble with John Pope had failed.

McClellan Takes Command

Pope had received reinforcements from McClellan's Army of the Potomac, principally V Corps commanded by Major General Fitz-John Porter, but it had not prevented his defeat at Second Manassas.

▶ *The Battle of Chantilly, 1 September 1862, ended the Second Manassas campaign with defeat for the North, marked by the death of the brave soldier, Union general Philip Kearny, shown here, and allowed Lee to take the offensive again.*

The Lincoln administration had not been pleased with the outcome of McClellan's Peninsular Campaign, which failed to take the rebel capital at Richmond, nor had the President appreciated 'Little Mac's' persistent call for more troops; so Lincoln had formed a new army under Pope for a fresh offensive. The War Department had ordered formations away from the Army of the Potomac at such a rate that McClellan began to believe himself 'in command of nothing more than my headquarters escort'. That had been before Pope's defeat at Second Manassas, and now Robert E. Lee apparently was leading a twice victorious rebel army on Washington.

The day of the engagement at Chantilly, 1 September, McClellan received verbal orders from President Lincoln to assume command of Washington, its defences and all forces in the immediate vicinity. This order was confirmed in writing from the Adjutant General's Office on 2 September 1862. Major General McClellan was ordered by the Government to display his considerable organizational talents, to return the Armies of Virginia and of the Potomac to fighting condition, and to save the Federal Capital. George Brinton McClellan believed that he was being called upon by an ungrateful administration to 'save the republic for a second time'. He rode out to meet Pope's returning troops. They were told that McClellan was again in command, and the effect was astonishing. Captain William H. Powell, serving then with the 4th United States Infantry Regiment in V Corps, recalled twenty four years later the dramatic impact this news had upon Pope's formations in the summer of 1862: 'Shout upon shout went out into the stillness of the night; and, as it was taken up along

▼ *Lightly equipped infantrymen under 'Stonewall' Jackson cross the Potomac River into Maryland at White's Ford.*

the road & repeated by regiment, brigade, division, and corps, we could hear the roar dying away in the distance. The effect of this man's presence upon the Army of the Potomac in sunshine or rain, in darkness or in daylight, in victory or defeat, was ever electrical and too wonderful to make it worthwhile attempting to give a reason for it.'

The Armies of Virginia and of the Potomac were consolidated as of 5 September. Major General John Pope was relieved from the command of troops, and all Federal forces in the immediate vicinity of Washington were placed under the command of Major General George McClellan. The geographic extent of McClellan's command was, however, somewhat uncertain. Major General Henry Halleck, acting as President Lincoln's chief of staff, apparently assumed that when a field force was again assembled to move against Robert E. Lee's Confederate Army of Northern Virginia some general other than McClellan would lead it. The Federal Government never had the time to consider the matter, for Lee's formations had begun crossing the Potomac River near Leesburg, Virginia, into Maryland the previous day, 4 September. McClellan was never appointed formally to the command of the field army defending the Federal Capital, a fact that explains to some extent his caution during the Maryland Campaign. McClellan wrote after the War: 'As the time had now arrived for the Army to advance, and I had received no written orders to take command of it, but had been expressly told that the assignment of a commander had not been decided, I determined to solve the question for myself.... I was afterwards accused of assuming command without authority, for nefarious purposes, and, in effect, fought the battles of South Mountain and Antietam with a halter around my neck; for if the Army of the Potomac had been defeated and I had survived I would, no doubt, have been tried for assuming authority without orders.'

McClellan assumed command of the field forces covering the capital, which advanced towards the enemy on 5 September. It consisted of I Corps (Hooker), II Corps (Sumner), 1st Division/IV Corps (attached to the VI Corps), V Corps (Porter), VI Corps (Franklin), IX Corps (Burnside), XII Corps (Mansfield) and a cavalry division (Pleasonton). McClellan divided his forces into a right wing under Major General Ambrose Burnside, consisting of I and IX Corps, a centre division under Major General Edwin Sumner of II and XII Corps, a left wing formed by VI Corps commanded by Major General William Franklin, and a reserve employing V Corps led by Major General Fitz-John Porter. Major General Nathaniel P. Banks was left in command of the defences of Washington with III Corps (Heintzelman), XI Corps (Sigel), and various garrison formations comprising XXII Corps.

Lee's Invasion of Maryland

The Army of the Potomac moved into Maryland. 'It was awful hot and tedious,' recalled Corporal Harrison Woodford of I Company/16th Connecticut Volunteers. 'The dust was half a foot deep,' he told his brother back home. It was the first field experience for the 16th Connecticut, and Corporal Woodford added in a letter dated 10 September, after further difficult marching following Lee into Maryland: 'A Soldier's life is a hard old life to lead, but I think I can ride it through. No one knows anything of the hardships of a soldier's life until they know it by experience.' Woodford's comment might stand for all soldiers, in all the campaigns of history.

The common soldiers in Robert E. Lee's Confederate Army of Northern Virginia were, if anything, more fatigued than their opponents. Lee had given his army no rest following the Second Manassas Campaign, and now he was leading it in a counter-offensive into Maryland. The southern commander was asking a great deal from tired flesh in that September of 1862. He considered it necessary to maintain offensive momentum, to keep the Federal forces off balance, and to prevent their occupation of as much of his beloved Virginia as he could manage. In addition, there were important political reasons for a Confederate offensive. The Confederate government assumed that there were large numbers of southern supporters in Maryland, and that the state was being held in the Federal union by force alone. 'If it is ever desired to give material aid to Maryland,' wrote Robert E. Lee to President Jefferson Davis on 3 September, 'and afford her an opportunity of throwing off the oppression to which she is now subject, this would seem the most favorable.' Southern political leaders thought that a large victorious southern army, Lee's army, moving into Maryland might gain that state for the Confederacy.

There was also a southern offensive being conducted in the western theatre. Confederate forces led by General Braxton Bragg and Major General Edmund Kirby Smith were invading Kentucky. Richmond entertained the same ambitions in the 'Blue Grass State' that it had in Maryland. The trump card would be a definite Southern military success in either or both Maryland and Kentucky. A

Southern military success in territory clearly *Northern*. The Confederate government believed that such an event would ensure European recognition of the Confederacy as a legitimate nation. The South might then receive serious foreign military assistance, as the American colonies had from France in the American Revolution. Confederate military resources were being strained to produce offensive movements in September 1862, for the South was gambling on the economic power of 'King Cotton' and potential battlefield victories in

A. P. Hill (left) with Robert E. Lee wearing Confederate generals' uniform. That of Hill is regulation, complete with forage cap; Lee later adopted a laydown collar instead of the stand-up version seen here; he wears no symbol of rank other than the stars on his collar. Painting by Ron Volstad.

Maryland and Kentucky. The risk for the South was great, but the stakes were high.

Special Order 191

General Robert E. Lee proposed to detach Major General Thomas J. 'Stonewall' Jackson with six divisions (McLaws, R. H. Anderson, Walker, Lawton, J. R. Jones and A. P. Hill), for the capture of the Federal garrison at Harper's Ferry. Major General James Longstreet would lead the general advance towards Hagerstown, Maryland, with two divisions, (D. R. Jones and Hood); while D. H. Hill's division, generally under Longstreet's command, guarded the right and rear of the advancing Confederate army. After the reduction of Harper's Ferry, Lee intended to continue the forward movement towards Harrisburg, Pennsylvania, threatening Baltimore, Philadelphia, or Washington as circumstances might seem to indicate. Lee was committing two-thirds of his army to the Harper's Ferry operation, and was considerably dividing his forces. The

---

Headquarters, Army of Northern Virginia
Sept, 9, 1862.

Special Orders, No. 191.

The army will resume its march to-morrow, taking the Hagerstown road. Gen. Jackson's command will form the advance, and after passing Middletown, with such portion as he may select, will take the route towards Sharpsburg, cross the Potomac at the most convenient point, and by Friday night take possession of the Baltimore and Ohio Railroad, capture such of the enemy as may be at Martinsburg, and intercept such as may attempt to escape from Harper's Ferry.

Gen. Longstreet's command will pursue the same road as far as Boonsborough, where it will halt with the reserve, supply, and baggage trains of the army.

Gen. McLaws, with his own division and that of Gen. R. H. Anderson, will follow Gen. Longstreet; on reaching Middletown he will take the route to Harper's Ferry, and by Friday morning possess himself of the Maryland Heights and endeavor to capture the enemy at Harper's Ferry and vicinity.

Gen. Walker, with his division, after accomplishing the object in which he is now engaged, will cross the Potomac at Cheek's ford, ascend its right bank to Lovettsville, take possession of Loudon Heights, if practicable, by Friday morning; Key's Ford on his left, and the road between the end of the mountain and the Potomac on his right. He will, as far as practicable, co-operate with Gen. McLaws and Gen. Jackson in intercepting the retreat of the enemy.

Gen. D. H. Hill's division will form the rear-guard of the army, pursuing the road taken by the main body. The reserve artillery, ordnance, and supply trains, etc., will precede Gen. Hill.

Gen. Stuart will detach a squadron of cavalry to accompany the commands of Gens. Longstreet, Jackson, and McLaws, and, with the main body of the cavalry, will cover the route of the army and bring up all stragglers that may have been left behind.

The commands of Gens. Jackson, McLaws, and Walker, after accomplishing the objects for which they have been detached, will join the main body of the army at Boonsborough or Hagerstown.

Each regiment on the march will habitually carry its axes in the regimental ordnance-wagons, for the use of the men at their encampments, to procure wood, etc.

By command of Gen. R. E. Lee

R. H. Chilton,
Assist. Adj.-Gen.

Major-Gen. D. H. Hill,
Commanding Division.

Confederate army was taking a chance, but Lee reasoned that after their defeat at Second Manassas the Federals would not move quickly, particularly if McClellan was in command. Lee issued Special Order 191, therefore, at Frederick, Maryland, on 9 September, detailing this operational plan. It contained the specific locations of Lee's formations for the next few days and clearly stated Lee's general intentions. He ordered that all his division commanders receive copies for their guidance while major portions of the Army of Northern Virginia operated separately.

The Federal army entered Frederick on 12 September, the same day that the siege of Harper's Ferry was commenced by Jackson's forces. The next morning private soldiers of the 27th Indiana Volunteers, camped on ground recently used by Daniel Harvey Hill's Confederate division, found a copy of Special Order 191 wrapped around some cigars. They realized the importance of their discovery, and by afternoon McClellan was in possession of General Lee's entire plan of operations. The astonishing carelessness, or more darkly the treachery of some Confederate staff officer now lost to history, had presented the commander of the Army of

▲ *After finding the orders that indicated how Lee's men would be distributed, McClellan finally led his army west to catch the Confederates off guard.*

Here he takes the salute of adoring civilians in Frederick City, Maryland, 12 September 1862. His advance would, however, be too slow.

the Potomac with the intelligence necessary to destroy Lee's army in detail before it could concentrate. The captured intelligence caused McClellan to move swiftly – far more swiftly than Lee could have imagined. He ordered the Federal army to force the passes over the South Mountain range of the Blue Ridge through Crampton's Gap, and through Turner's Gap and its subsidiary, Fox's Gap. McClellan would move on Boonsboro, interposing his army between the forces of Jackson at Harper's Ferry and Longstreet near Hagerstown. But McClellan did not move swiftly enough, and historians have castigated him for not ordering a night march on the thirteenth. It would be morning on 14 September before the Army of the Potomac was in position opposite the key South Mountain positions.

Lee was made aware by a citizen of Southern sympathies on the evening of 13 September of the

disastrous news that McClellan was in possession of Special Order 191. The Army of Northern Virginia was dangerously separated, the reduction of Harper's Ferry was in hand, but not completed; and McClellan was on the move fully informed of Lee's intentions. Lee ordered an immediate withdrawal south of the Potomac River. He also instructed Longstreet to support D. H. Hill's division deployed to cover the passes McClellan must use to divide the Confederate army. The stage was set for the engagements of Crampton's Gap and Turner's Gap, known collectively as South Mountain, fought on 14 September 1862.

◀ *Major General John G. Walker's division took possession of Loudoun Heights at Harper's Ferry as McClellan was closing in on Lee's Army. Yet Walker and his men would manage to march to Sharpsburg in time to be of tremendous service.*

▼ *Walker's troops held a commanding position on Loudoun Heights which are, as seen in this wartime sketch, the dominating position near Harper's Ferry.*

The Approaches to South Mountain, 13 to 14 Sept 1862

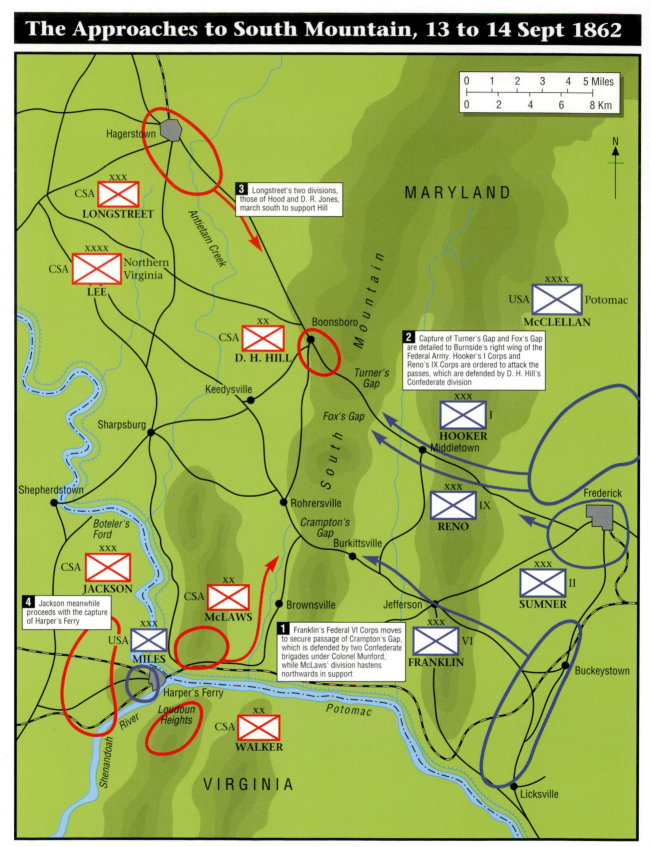

3 Longstreet's two divisions, those of Hood and D. R. Jones, march south to support Hill

MARYLAND

CSA LONGSTREET

CSA Northern Virginia LEE

Antietam Creek

Hagerstown

CSA D. H. HILL

Boonsboro

Keedysville

Turner's Gap

Fox's Gap

Sharpsburg

USA Potomac McCLELLAN

2 Capture of Turner's Gap and Fox's Gap are detailed to Burnside's right wing of the Federal Army. Hooker's I Corps and Reno's IX Corps are ordered to attack the passes, which are defended by D. H. Hill's Confederate division

Mountain

South

HOOKER I

Middletown

Frederick

RENO IX

Shepherdstown

Boteler's Ford

Rohrersville

Crampton's Gap

Burkittsville

SUMNER II

CSA JACKSON

4 Jackson meanwhile proceeds with the capture of Harper's Ferry

CSA McLAWS

Brownsville

Jefferson

FRANKLIN VI

1 Franklin's Federal VI Corps moves to secure passage of Crampton's Gap, which is defended by two Confederate brigades under Colonel Munford, while McLaws' division hastens northwards in support

Buckeystown

USA MILES

Harper's Ferry

Loudoun Heights

River

Shenandoah

CSA WALKER

Potomac

Licksville

VIRGINIA

N

| 0 | 1 | 2 | 3 | 4 | 5 Miles |
| 0 | 2 | 4 | 6 | 8 Km |

THE OPPOSING COMMANDERS

An analysis of the two army commanders, Major General George McClellan leading the Federal Army of the Potomac and General Robert E. Lee commanding the Confederate Army of Northern Virginia, reveals that the two shared common backgrounds. They possessed a common education, had experienced similar military careers, and represented the upper levels of American society. They were personally known to each other, having served together during the War with Mexico (1846–7) on the engineering staff of Major General Winfield Scott, and both respected the military abilities of the other. Lee remarked after the end of the war that McClellan was the most dangerous opponent he had faced. Lee suggested that McClellan was, in an academic sense, the most professional leader of the Army of the Potomac. McClellan wrote in his memoirs concerning Lee: 'I had the highest respect for his ability as a commander, and knew that he was not a general to be trifled with or carelessly afforded an opportunity of striking a fatal blow.'

The Federal Commanders

George Brinton McClellan was born into a rather prestigious family, with colonial New England roots, at Philadelphia, Pennsylvania, on 3 December 1826. The son of a prominent physician, McClellan initially attended the University of Pennsylvania, but entered the United States Military Academy at West Point in 1842. The curriculum at West Point in McClellan's day did not include a great deal of military history. McClellan was president of an undergraduate society, however, that met during the cadet's free time and was dedicated to the study of Napoleon and his military operations. He graduated second in the class of 1846, and as an officer of engineers he went immediately to the war with Mexico. McClellan won three brevets for gallantry and sound professional services during this conflict.

He was sent abroad to investigate European military academies and was a military observer during the Crimean War. In addition, McClellan found time to design a saddle for American mounted formations and to write a small book on bayonet drill. He was clearly an officer truly interested in his profession. McClellan was a captain in the 1st United States Cavalry in 1857, when he resigned to become chief engineer on the Illinois Central Railroad. The beginning of the American Civil War found him president of the Ohio and Mississippi Railroad.

McClellan received high rank early in the war. He directed a successful campaign in West Virginia and was called upon by the Lincoln administration to reorganize the Federal forces before Washington, D.C., following McDowell's defeat in the First Manassas Campaign. George McClellan was an excellent administrative officer, a splendid organizer of armies and a superb drillmaster. The republic owed him a great deal for forging the instrument that would ultimately defeat the rebellion. He also possessed sound strategic sense. The general conception of the 1862 Peninsular Campaign was illustrative of McClellan's considerable strategic abilities. He demonstrated repeatedly, however, that his tactical direction on the battlefield was overly conservative and characterized by extreme caution. McClellan tended to overestimate the numbers available to his opponent. And, while he was able to generate intense loyalty from his subordinates, he clashed with his military equals and consistently failed to work in harmony with his political superiors.

The Army of the Potomac retained high confidence in McClellan despite these deficiencies. He had nearly taken Richmond in the summer of 1862, and the officers and men of the army were convinced the rebel capital would have fallen had there not been interference by the Lincoln administration. The failure to destroy Lee's army at Antietam

◀ Major General Joseph Hooker was to earn command of the Army of the Potomac after McClellan was dismissed, in large part because of his aggressive attacks at Antietam, as I Corps commander, which opened the battle.

▶ Major General Ambrose Burnside allowed his command to become entangled at the bridge that thereafter forever would bear his name, and failed to hit the Confederate Army at the same time as other commands were attacking along the line.

would not shake this confidence; indeed, the caution McClellan displayed and for which he has been criticized by generations of historians accounted for some of his popularity. Captain Charles Francis Adams, of the 1st Massachusetts Volunteer Cavalry, commented with perceptive insight upon McClellan's removal from command of the Army of the Potomac following the Maryland Campaign: 'We believed in him, not as a brilliant commander, but as a prudent one and one who was gradually learning how to handle our immense army, and now a new man must learn and he must learn by his own mistakes and in the blood of the army.' The Army of the Potomac was very much 'McClellan's Army' in the first two years of the war.

Of the the corps commanders at Antietam, the actions of those at each flank were to have sirnificant repercussions on the course of the battle.

On the right flank, Federal I Corps was commanded by Joseph Hooker (1814–79), an 1837 graduate of the United States Military Academy, who had served in the Mexican War before resigning in

1853 to farm. He offered his services at the beginning of the Civil War, commanding a brigade, a division and eventually a corps with credit. Hooker was flamboyant, aggressive and ambitious. He made good newspaper copy, the reporters tagged him 'Fighting Joe' during the Peninsular Campaign, and although he would fail as an army commander during the May 1863 Chancellorsville Campaign, he displayed competence at Lookout Mountain in November 1863 and displayed consistently sound tactical ability while commanding XX Corps in the Army of the Cumberland during Sherman's 1864 Atlanta Campaign.

It was rumoured that Hooker drank to excess and that he liked the ladies. Hooker acquired quite a reputation for personal immorality early in the War, causing one well brought up Massachusetts officer serving on his staff to reply to his sister's request that she be allowed to visit him during the winter, 'General Hooker's headquarters is a place that no lady could visit with propriety.' The newspaper reporters jokingly suggested that the large numbers

blockading fleet, staging areas for future assaults on southern railroad lines supplying Virginia, and would succeed in denying much of North Carolina to the Confederacy for the remainder of the War. Burnside secured for himself a reputation as a successful independent commander, and he looked the part. 'I have seen old Burnside,' wrote Harrison Woodford of the 16th Connecticut to his sister Mattie, 'He is a stern resolute looking man.'

The Confederate Commanders

In a similar fashion to the Federal Army of the Potomac, the Confederate Army of Northern Virginia became 'Lee's Army' in the minds of many following the assumption of command by Robert E. Lee after the wounding of General Joseph E. Johnston on the first day (31 May 1862), of the engagement of Seven Pines or Fair Oaks. Lee directed next a series of offensive battles known as the Seven Days, designed to drive McClellan's Army of the Potomac away from Richmond. He then defeated John Pope's Army of Virginia in a convincing fashion in the Second Manassas Campaign. The officers and men of the Army of Northern Virginia quickly developed supreme confidence in Lee's leadership abilities. Robert E. Lee received intense loyalty from his army, but Lee also received from his men what few generals experience – an emotional devotion to his person.

Robert Edward Lee was born 19 January 1807 into one of Virginia's most aristocratic families. His father, Henry 'Light Horse Harry' Lee (1756–1818), was a famous continental cavalry officer during the American Revolution, one of the members of the first American Congress and eventually governor of Virginia. Robert Lee entered West Point in 1825 and graduated second in his class in 1829 without receiving a single demerit for conduct deficiencies. He served in the corps of engineers constructing coastal fortifications and served on Winfield Scott's staff during the 1847 drive on Mexico City. Lee won three brevet promotions in Mexico and a reputation as one of the most able officers in the entire army. He served as Superintendent of the United States Military Academy at West Point between 1852 and 1855. His superintendency is regarded as one of the most suc-

of prostitutes flocking to Washington in 1861 constituted 'Hooker's Division'. It is a name that has stuck to street walkers ever since. Joe Hooker was perhaps not a man one might introduce to polite society at a fashionable dinner on Beacon Hill in Boston, but he was the man McClellan trusted with commencing the destruction of Lee's Army. It would prove a difficult task.

At the other end of the Federal line would stand the Federal IX Corps, under the command of Ambrose Everett Burnside (1824–81). He was an 1847 graduate of the United States Military Academy, and a veteran of the war with Mexico. Burnside left the regular army in 1857 to manufacture a breech-loading carbine of his own invention. He led the 1st Rhode Island Volunteers at First Manassas and engineered the successful occupation of the Outer Banks coastal area of North Carolina. Burnside's North Carolina expedition in the early months of 1862 produced victories for the North at Roanoke Island, Fort Macon, and at New Berne. It also secured valuable anchorages for the Federal

General Robert E. Lee, in command of the Army of Northern Virginia for less than a year, took a major gamble in bringing the war to Maryland, partly because of a mistaken impression that Marylanders would flock to the Southern cause.

cessful in West Point's history. Lee was lieutenant colonel of the newly raised 2nd United States Cavalry, fighting Indians on the western plains from 1855 – this, it should be noted, being Lee's only experience leading troops before the Civil War.

The growing sectional difficulties that brought about the American Civil War were made apparent to Lee in 1859, when he commanded the detachment of troops that captured John Brown's men at Harper's Ferry, Virginia. Lee was offered high command in the Federal army early in the war, but he declined out of loyalty to Virginia. He commanded briefly in the western sections of Virginia, completed an inspection tour of Confederate eastern coastal defences, and was serving as President Jefferson Davis's military adviser when he assumed command of the troops defending Richmond.

Lee nearly achieved sainthood status in the years following 1865, as the South needed a hero to help deal with the humiliation suffered by defeat.

Americans have never accepted military defeat well. Lee has been defended by generations of loyal Southern historians, and it is only recently that some of his defects have been studied. Lee consistently failed to appreciate the complete military picture; rather he tended to look at the conflict only as it impacted upon his own theatre in Virginia. This is natural enough, but Lee's growing reputation gained as a result of impressive but strategically barren victories in Virginia precluded the Confederacy from deploying adequate resources in the western theatre. Tactically, Lee persisted in employing outdated Napoleonic infantry assaults when growing evidence suggested the sterility of such tactics. The South could not afford the casualties suffered as a result of such frontal assaults as Lee launched at Malvern Hill and Gettysburg. Lee generally failed to give precise orders to his subordinate commanders and failed to understand how to delegate authority. His staff officers, commenting on Lee's insistence upon having a say in even the most minute matters of army business, called him behind his back 'the Tycoon'.

In addition to these characteristics, Lee was often in poor health. With perceived heart troubles, he frequently expressed the opinion that he would not survive the war. During the Maryland Campaign Lee was suffering from intense pain in his hands, as a result of an accident that took place on 2 September. He had dismounted to speak with Longstreet and his staff. His horse was startled and jumped backwards, while Lee held the horse's bridle loosely in his hands. Thrown violently to the ground, Lee sprained both wrists and broke a number of bones in his hands while attempting to stop his fall. As a result the Confederate commander was unable to write, rode with difficulty, and frequently travelled in an ambulance during the Maryland operations.

Lee was an able field commander. He had the full confidence of his troops. His officers were convinced that wherever Lee led, victories like Second Manassas would follow. Defeat was perceived only as temporary setback and nothing dulled the unbounded confidence the Army of Northern Virginia had in Lee throughout the remainder of the war. How many commanders of armies have fought their campaigns with such devotion and con-

Lieutenant General Thomas J. Jackson with almost half of the Confederate army was well to the west, capturing the garrison at Harper's Ferry, Virginia, during the opening phase of the Antietam campaign.

Major General James Longstreet won promotion to lieutenant general (9 October 1862) in large part because of his activities at Sharpsburg. Foot problems caused him to have to wear slippers instead of boots during the battle itself.

fidence? The South expected great things of the army Lee had forged.

The capture of Harper's Ferry and the critical battle on the Confederate left at Antietam would be entrusted to 'Stonewall' Jackson. Thomas Jonathan Jackson (1824–63), an 1846 graduate of the United States Military Academy, had won three brevets for gallantry during the war with Mexico, while serving with the new 'flying artillery'. He taught Natural Philosophy and Artillery Tactics at the Virginia Military Institute from 1851, and the cadets did not like him. Jackson was not an imaginative instructor. He would memorize each day's lesson the night before and simply repeat it in class; and if a cadet had the temerity to ask a question Jackson would start the lecture again from the beginning. Jackson was a strict disciplinarian, insisting on the exact limit of the regulations, and he was famous for the number of court-martial proceedings he initiated against cadets. The cadets called him 'Tom Fool

Jackson' and 'Old Blue Light', making fun of the stern major when opportunity presented itself. For example, on one occasion Jackson was trying to teach the mobile artillery tactics he had learned in Mexico, and in the absence of horses he placed cadets to draw the guns, caissons and limbers. Jackson ordered the cadets to trot, and one cadet in a lead position refused to move. He placed the offending cadet under arrest. During the court-martial proceedings, when asked why he had refused to move forward after Major Jackson's order, the cadet responded by stating: 'Sir, Major Jackson ordered me to trot. I am a natural pacer.'

The VMI Board of Visitors considered dispensing with Jackson's services. He was not even on speaking terms with the school's superintendent, Colonel Francis Henney Smith, but no one could deny the man's obvious ability with field pieces; and when the VMI Corps of Cadets went to Richmond in 1861 to train Virginia's regiments the battalion of

Major General Ambrose Powell Hill forced his men in a desperate march to reach Lee's force at Sharpsburg, arriving late in the day to turn the tide and force an end to Federal attacks.

cadets marched behind Major Jackson. Jackson acquired the famous sobriquet 'Stonewall' at First Manassas in July 1861 and conducted the magnificent Shenandoah Valley Campaign in 1862, perhaps one of the most successful strategic diversions in all military history. Jackson fumbled to a degree as a somewhat independent offensive commander during Lee's Seven Days operations against McClellan on the Peninsula, but he had performed admirably during the Second Manassas Campaign and during the early stages of the Maryland Campaign.

Other key commanders at Antietam included Brigadier General John Bell Hood (1831–79). A graduate of the United States Military Academy, he had served with Lee before the War fighting Indians in the 2nd United States Cavalry. John Hood was perhaps one of the most aggressive combat officers in either army. He was an excellent divisional leader on the battlefield, although he possessed only a very limited knowledge of logistics, and he would fail dismally in 1864 as commander of the Confederate

Army of Tennessee. At Antietam, however, he was to play a decisive part in halting the attack of Hooker's Federal I Corps.

The struggle for the sunken road – 'Bloody Lane' – would involve hard fighting by the command of Daniel Harvey Hill (1821–89), an 1842 graduate of the United States Military Academy and Jackson's brother-in-law. He had won two brevets in Mexico, but resigned in 1849 to become a professor of mathematics. A difficult subordinate, he was not an easy man to get along with, and convinced that there was too much 'Virginian influence' in Lee's army. No one would have denied, however, that he was a splendid fighter, perhaps the best division commander in the Army of Northern Virginia.

At the southern end of the Confederate line at Antietam, all would ultimately depend upon the division of Ambrose Powell Hill (1825–65). He was an 1847 graduate of the United States Military Academy and a veteran of both the Mexican and Seminole wars. Hill had demonstrated a hard driving, aggressive style of divisional leadership in the campaigns previous to the Maryland operations. Although he often feuded with his superiors, he was widely regarded as the best divisional commander in the Confederate Army.

▶ *Northerners could not figure out how Confederate troops could fight so well for an obviously bad cause. This piece of Northern propaganda attempts to explain it by indicating that they had to fight or be killed by their own officers and provost guards, who were posted in the rear during battle to stop straggling.*

THE OPPOSING ARMIES

The American Civil War was fought basically with volunteer regiments. The regular Army of the United States in 1860 consisted only of ten regiments of infantry, four regiments of artillery, two regiments of dragoons, the regiment of mounted rifles, and two regiments of cavalry. In the early months of the conflict the Federal government added a regiment of cavalry and renumbered all the mounted regiments (the 1st and 2nd Dragoons, the Regiment of Mounted Rifles, the 1st, 2nd, and 3rd Cavalry retitled respectively, the 1st, 2nd, 3rd, 4th, 5th, and 6th Cavalry). The War Department also created another regiment of artillery and nine new regular regiments, each to consist of three battalions of eight companies (the older regiments remaining each a single battalion of ten companies).

There were a number of proposals as to how the small regular army might be best employed. Some

argued that the formations should be broken up and the personnel assigned to the new volunteer formations: the men promoted noncommissioned officers, the noncommissioned officers promoted line officers, the line officers promoted field officers, and the field officers promoted to general rank. A plan very much like this had been drafted by John C. Calhoun when he had been Secretary of War during the administration of James Monroe. It was suggested that individual regular formations be assigned to volunteer brigades and divisions. This practice was followed more or less in the artillery, where one regular light battery was assigned to a volunteer artillery brigade. Major General (brevet Lieutenant General) Winfield Scott, commander in chief of the pre-war regular army, insisted that regular army formations, with the exception of the artillery, where the companies served independently as light artillery batteries throughout the conflict, be kept together as a final reserve. There were a substantial number of regular officers who, as a result of this decision, wished to leave their regiments to accept higher rank in the new volunteer formations, a practice encouraged by the various state governors, who realized the value of a regular subaltern drilling a new volunteer regiment as a field officer. The Federal War Department was very reluctant to allow this but was forced to do so ultimately by circumstance. There were a large number of Federal officers who held much higher volunteer rank than their regular rank during the war, a situation complicated further by the practice of granting brevet commissions in both the regular and volunteer service in reward for exemplary conduct.

A Federal volunteer regiment originated at the state level. State governors received requests from the Federal War Department on several occasions to provide a given number of regiments for Federal service. The governor would select a prominent individual he believed capable of gathering enough men for a regiment. The new colonel would then select ten individuals he believed able to raise a company. The remaining field officers were often appointed by the governor, although the wishes of the regiment in this matter were generally respected. Finally, all commissions were granted by the governor and later approved by the War Department in Washington. There were Federal officer boards that later examined the fitness of indi-

Lieutenant Colonel of the 9th New York Cavalry. In the field, the sash was rarely worn except by the officer of the day. Painting by Michael Youens.

vidual officers. The criteria for officer selection had less to do with military experience than with the position of the individual in pre-war society. The important thing was to attract men into the service. The duties of an infantry officer were not overly complicated in 1861, and a reasonably intelligent individual could learn them through diligent application to the army regulations and the various drill manuals. The new regiment was eventually inspected and mustered into the Federal service by a regular officer in each state detailed for this purpose. There was very little resembling modern basic training. The 14th Connecticut Volunteers, for example, went into the battle of Antietam without having been instructed in the operation of their rifles.

A regiment was fortunate to have a West Point graduate, an officer of the regular army, or even an officer of the pre-war militia as one of its field officers. The new volunteers did not take well to discipline, but they were splendid material and developed into veteran formations in an astonishingly short time. Field officers with regular experience found that their men resented attempts to employ 'old army' discipline. 'These regular officers,' wrote Horace H. Justis, Lieutenant and Adjutant of the 65th Ohio Volunteers, 'think a private is not as good as they.' Justis complained further about his regular army colonel: 'Thinks he knows everything and don't like to be advised. That style won't do. He will gradually be disliked by the regiment.'

The men discovered quickly, however, the value of such training. They discovered that seemingly odious methods saved lives on the battlefield and through adequate sanitation prevented deaths in camp. Isaac Ingalls Stevens started the war as colonel of the 79th New York Volunteers. He was an 1839 graduate of West Point and an officer of long military experience. Stevens was forced to stare down a mutiny with his revolver, after he had insisted on employing regular discipline with his New Yorkers. The men of the 79th New York, however, after they had served in several battles with Stevens, voluntarily gave up a month's pay to buy him a sword in appreciation of his leadership.

There were similar situations in Southern regiments. There were incompetent officers in both

▲ *Confederates in the Maryland Campaign were never as uniform or even well clad as these in* *a print of the attack over the Burnside Bridge made by Kurz and Allison years after the war.*

armies. North and South were saddled with generals selected for their political positions and with regular officers grown far too old in the service to fight another war. The majority of regular officers had vast experience with company size formations, but few had commanded anything larger; indeed, the Mexican War had been the last time large formations had been employed. Confederate Lieutenant General Richard Ewell remarked on his pre-war military experience by stating that he had 'learned everything there was to know about leading a company of dragoons, but nothing else'. The amazing thing is that so many competent and really very able generals were eventually found.

The soldier's home was his regiment or battery, which functioned much like a mobile community. There were ten companies in an infantry regiment, twelve companies in a regiment of cavalry, and light artillery batteries were grouped in battalions or brigades of three to five batteries from 1862. The basic tactical unit, however, was the brigade. The regiments in Southern brigades were frequently from the same state. This practice was less common in Northern armies. Formations were deployed in shoulder-to-shoulder fashion, despite the addition of rifled weapons to the battlefield; although both sides employed increasingly heavy skirmishing lines as the war progressed.

The armies were armed with a mix of smooth-bore and rifled weaponry. The notion that all Civil War soldiers carried rifled muskets is inaccurate; in fact, some brigades deliberately armed some regiments with smooth-bore muskets in order to fire 'buck and ball' as an anti-personnel round at close range. The situation in the artillery was similar, and although a number of different guns were used, the goal was a mix of rifled and smooth-bored artillery. The Federal Army of the Potomac, for example, used the 3in Ordnance Rifle for longer range work against other artillery, fortifications, or troops

deployed at a distance. The smooth-bored twelve-pounder 'Napoleon' was used for breaking up infantry assaults at close range with canister.

The employment of mounted formations in the American Civil War is a most interesting topic. There were mounted sabre charges on the European model, sometimes on a large scale, such as took place at Brandy Station and at Gettysburg. The armies often employed their mounted arm, however, in raiding operations and as a species of mounted infantry. The raid conducted by Colonel Benjamin Grierson in May 1863 with three regiments through the state of Mississippi represents perhaps the most successful mounted raid of the war, certainly the one operation that had the most strategic success. Raiding operations in general, however, proved to be a dissipation of military resources. Such operations were romantic but not very productive of long term results. General William Sherman once remarked that he had never seen cavalry destroy railroad track to such an extent as to make it unserviceable for more than four or five days. Brigadier General John Buford clearly demonstrated the great utility of cavalry as mounted infantry through his extremely successful holding action on the first day of the battle of Gettysburg with his 1st Division/Cavalry Corps/ Potomac.

▲ *An artillery battery gallops forward into action and prepares to open fire, apparently into a very thick 'fog of battle' according to this contemporary illustration.*

The Federal government was at first reluctant to raise volunteer cavalry regiments, considering them expensive and thinking that cavalry drill was too complicated to be assimilated by the volunteer in a short time. The War Department eventually raised substantial numbers of cavalry regiments. One of the errors McClellan committed during the Maryland Campaign was in failing to find use for his cavalry division. Brigadier General Alfred Pleasonton's men sat out the battle of Antietam, while a logical employment for them would have been to secure a crossing of the Antietam Creek downstream from Burnside's Bridge. The Confederate government raised more cavalry regiments than they could find horses for, and many Southern cavalry formations fought the war dismounted as infantry.

The actual number of men present with the armies during the Maryland Campaign is a matter of much debate. It is made complicated by the different book-keeping arrangements used at the time by the opposing sides. The issue was complicated further by post-war Southern political considerations. The Federal Army of the Potomac and all other Northern military organizations, required to submit monthly returns to the War Department in Washington, reported everyone attached to the various formations on the strength returns regardless of their current individual situation. The result was inflated, as men serving in a variety of extra duties, on leave, legitimately or illegitimately absent, temporarily sick or disabled, were reported as being actually present with their regiments. In addition, officers, musicians, and noncommissioned officers were included in the general total. The result is that Federal strength returns do not reflect accurately the number of men present on the battle line at any particular moment in time. The Southern practice was to list only those men who were actually present and only those men actually bearing a rifle in the battle line.

It became important in the post-war years for the defeated South to insist that Southern generalship was not the reason for Southern defeat, but rather chance and overwhelming Northern numbers. The post-war Southern political leadership had to explain military defeat if they were to resume their positions in the post-war South. Their argument seems to be supported by a comparison of Northern and Southern strength returns for a given battle. The simple truth is that on the battle line for much of the American Civil War at the point of contact numbers were more or less equal, with temporary fluctuating numerical advantage. When the North was on the offensive in a hostile country, it was necessary to detach formations to protect lines of communication the deeper a Federal army moved into Southern territory. The South being overwhelmed by huge numbers of Northern soldiers is a myth made more apparent than real by differing accounting systems and post-war Southern recollections motivated by political considerations.

The Army of Northern Virginia suffered throughout the Maryland Campaign from extreme straggling. The vast majority of Southern participants comment on the excessive number of men leaving the ranks. Common soldiers had varied reasons for failing to keep up with their regiments. Major General Daniel Harvey Hill wrote in his general report of operations in Maryland: 'Doubtless the want of shoes, the want of food, and physical exhaustion had kept many brave men from being with the army; but thousands of thieving poltroons had kept away from sheer cowardice.' There were also political reasons.

The South raised volunteer regiments early in the war in the same manner as their Northern opponents; however, the Confederacy resorted to a draft much earlier than the North. There were many Southern soldiers unhappy with the 1862 Confederate Conscription Act. Men who had enlisted for one year found to their surprise that under the terms of the Conscription Act their one-year regiment had instantly been converted to a regiment enlisted for the duration of the conflict, without their consent and without the opportunity to elect new officers. The Conscription Act seemed to place the Southern manpower burden on the economically disadvantaged, providing exemptions for slave owners and allowing the purchase of substitutes by those with financial means. The Act suggested the validity of the common adage that it was indeed 'a rich man's war, but a poor man's fight'. In addition, the Confederate government insisted that the conflict was necessary to protect the entirety of Southern culture and that a defensive war only would be prosecuted. The invasion of Maryland seemed contrary to the stated objectives of the Davis administration, and substantial elements of Lee's army expressed their political sentiments and their opinion of the Conscription Act through temporary desertion until the termination of the Maryland Campaign.

Honest estimates of the rank and file strength of Lee's Army of Northern Virginia present at Antietam range from 35,000 to 55,000. The approximate figure of 45,000 would seem fairly accurate. The estimates of McClellan's Army of the Potomac range from 79,000 to 90,000, although a figure of 82,000 is more accurate. It should be remembered that McClellan failed to employ all his available forces, fighting the battle of Antietam basically with I, II, IX, and XII Corps, perhaps 50,000 men or more. Lee was forced by circumstances to employ everyone present. The best that can be said with respect to numbers engaged is that Lee's Army was outnumbered at Antietam, although by exactly what margin is a matter of speculation.

ORDER OF BATTLE: UNITED STATES FORCES

Field Forces, Defences of Washington, Army of the Potomac
George Brinton McClellan, Major General USA

Escort: Oneida (New York) Volunteer Cavalry Co., A & E/ 4th US Regular Cavalry. Headquarters Guard: 93rd New York Volunteers. Provost & Quartermaster's Guard: BCH & I/ 1st US Regular Cavalry, EFH & K/ 2nd US Regular Cavalry, ADF & G/ 8th US Regular Infantry, G & H/ 19th US Regular Infantry

Unattached formations: US Regular Engineer Battalion

I CORPS
Joseph Hooker, Major General USV

Escort: ABI & K/ 2nd New York Volunteer Cavalry

1st Division
John Porter Hatch, Brigadier General USV
1st Brigade (Walter Phelps, Colonel 22nd New York Volunteers): 22nd, 24th, 30th, 84th New York Volunteers (14th New York Militia), 2nd US Volunteers Sharpshooters
2nd Brigade (Abner Doubleday, Brigadier General USV): 7th Indiana Volunteers, 76th, 95th New York Volunteers, 56th Pennsylvania Volunteers
3rd Brigade (Marsena Rudolph Patrick, Brigadier General USV): 21st, 23rd, 35th, 80th New York Volunteers (20th New York Militia)
4th Brigade (The Iron Brigade) (John Gibbon, Brigadier General USV): 19th Indiana Volunteers, 2nd, 6th, 7th Wisconsin Volunteers
Artillery: B/4th US Regular Artillery, D/1st Rhode Island Volunteer Artillery, L/1st New York Volunteer Artillery, 1st Independent Battery, New Hampshire Volunteer Light Artillery

2nd Division
James Brewerton Ricketts, Brigadier General USV
1st Brigade (Abram Duryee, Brigadier General USV): 97th, 104th, 105th New York Volunteers, 107th Pennsylvania Volunteers

2nd Brigade (William Henry Christian, Colonel 26th New York Volunteers): 26th, 94th New York Volunteers, 88th, 90th Pennsylvania Volunteers
3rd Brigade (George Lucas Hartsuff, Brigadier General USV): 16th Maine Volunteers (detached as railroad guard 13 Sept.), 12th, 13th Massachusetts Volunteers, 83rd New York Volunteers (9th New York Militia), 11th Pennsylvania Volunteers
Artillery: F/1st Pennsylvania Volunteer Artillery, C/ Pennsylvania Volunteer Light Artillery

3rd Division
George Gordon Meade, Brigadier General USV
1st Brigade (Truman Seymour, Brigadier General USV): 1st Pennsylvania Reserves (30th Pennsylvania Volunteers), 2nd Pennsylvania Reserves (31st Pennsylvania Volunteers), 5th Pennsylvania Reserves (34th Pennsylvania Volunteers), 6th Pennsylvania Reserves (35th Pennsylvania Volunteers), 13th Pennsylvania Reserves (42nd Pennsylvania Volunteers)
2nd Brigade (Albert Magilton, Colonel): 3rd Pennsylvania Reserves (32nd Pennsylvania Volunteers), 4th Pennsylvania Reserves (33rd Pennsylvania Volunteers), 7th Pennsylvania Reserves (36th Pennsylvania Volunteers), 8th Pennsylvania Reserves (37th Pennsylvania Volunteers)
3rd Brigade (Thomas Foster Gallagher, Colonel 11th Pennsylvania Reserves): 9th Pennsylvania Reserves (38th Pennsylvania Volunteers), 10th Pennsylvania Reserves (39th Pennsylvania Volunteers), 11th Pennsylvania Reserves (40th Pennsylvania Volunteers), 12th Pennsylvania Reserves (41st Pennsylvania Volunteers)
Artillery: C/5th US Regular Artillery, A/1st Pennsylvania Volunteer Artillery, B/1st Pennsylvania Volunteer Artillery, G/1st Pennsylvania Volunteer Artillery (detached at Washington 6 Sept.)

II CORPS
Edwin Vose Sumner, Major General USV
Escort: D & K/6th New York

Volunteer Cavalry

1st Division
Israel Bush Richardson, Brigadier General USV
1st Brigade (John Curtis Caldwell, Brigadier General USV): 5th New Hampshire Volunteers, 7th New York Volunteers, 61st & 64th New York Volunteers, 81st Pennsylvania Volunteers
2nd Brigade (The Irish Brigade) (Thomas Francis Meagher, Brigadier General USV): 29th Massachusetts Volunteers, 63rd New York Volunteers, 69th New York Volunteers, 88th New York Volunteers
3rd Brigade (John Rutter Brooke, Colonel 53rd Pennsylvania Volunteers): 2nd Delaware Volunteers, 52nd New York Volunteers, 57th New York Volunteers, 66th New York Volunteers, 53rd Pennsylvania Volunteers
Artillery: A & C/4th US Regular Artillery, B/1st New York Volunteer Artillery

2nd Division
John Sedgwick, Major General USV
1st Brigade (Willis Arnold Gorman, Brigadier General USV): 15th Massachusetts Volunteers, 1st Minnesota Volunteers, 34th New York Volunteers, 82nd New York Volunteers (2nd New York Militia), 1st Company Massachusetts Sharpshooters, 2nd Company Minnesota Sharpshooters
2nd Brigade (The Philadelphia Brigade) (Oliver Otis Howard, Brigadier General USV): 69th Pennsylvania Volunteers, 71st Pennsylvania Volunteers, 72nd Pennsylvania Volunteers, 106th Pennsylvania Volunteers
3rd Brigade (Napoleon Jackson Tecumseh Dana, Brigadier General USV): 19th Massachusetts Volunteers, 20th Massachusetts Volunteers, 7th Michigan Volunteers, 42nd New York Volunteers, 59th New York Volunteers
Artillery: I/1st US Regular Artillery, A/1st Rhode Island Volunteer Artillery

3rd Division
William Henry French, Brigadier

General USV

1ST BRIGADE (Nathan Kimball, Brigadier General USV): 14th Indiana Volunteers, 8th Ohio Volunteers, 132nd Pennsylvania Volunteers, 7th West Virginia Volunteers

2ND BRIGADE (Dwight Morris, Colonel 14th Connecticut Volunteers): 14th Connecticut Volunteers, 108th New York Volunteers, 130th Pennsylvania Volunteers

3RD BRIGADE (Max Weber, Brigadier General USV): 1st Delaware Volunteers, 5th Maryland Volunteers, 4th New York Volunteers

ARTILLERY: G/1st New York Volunteer Artillery, B/1st Rhode Island Volunteer Artillery, G/1st Rhode Island Volunteer Artillery

V CORPS

Fitz-John Porter, Major General USV
Escort: 1st Maine Volunteer Cavalry (detachment)

1ST DIVISION

George Webb Morell, Brigadier General USV

1ST BRIGADE (James Barnes, Colonel 18th Massachusetts Volunteers): 2nd Maine Volunteers, 18th Massachusetts Volunteers, 22nd Massachusetts Volunteers, 1st Michigan Volunteers, 13th New York Volunteers, 25th New York Volunteers, 118th Pennsylvania Volunteers, 2nd Company, Massachusetts Volunteer Sharpshooters

2ND BRIGADE (Charles Griffin, Brigadier General USV): 2nd District of Columbia Volunteers, 9th Massachusetts Volunteers, 32nd Massachusetts Volunteers, 4th Michigan Volunteers, 14th New York Volunteers, 62nd Pennsylvania Volunteers

3RD BRIGADE (T.B.W. Stockton, Colonel): 20th Maine Volunteers, 16th Michigan Volunteers, 12th New York Volunteers, 17th New York Volunteers, 44th New York Volunteers, 83rd Pennsylvania Volunteers, Brady's Company of Michigan Volunteer Sharpshooters

ARTILLERY: D/5th US Regular Artillery, 3rd Independent Battery, Massachusetts Volunteer Light Artillery, C/1st Rhode Island Volunteer Artillery

Soldier of the 14th Brooklyn Regiment, still wearing the pre-war red trousers; for most units, these were replaced in time by standard Union fatigue dress. Painting by Michael Youens.

2ND DIVISION

George Sykes, Brigadier General USV

1ST BRIGADE (Robert Christie Buchanan, Lt. Colonel 4th US Regular Infantry): 3rd US Regular Infantry, 4th US Regular Infantry, I/12th US Regular Infantry, II/12th US Regular Infantry, I/14th US Regular Infantry, II/14th US Regular Infantry

2ND BRIGADE (Charles Swain Lovell, Major 10th US Regular Infantry): 1st & 6th US Regular Infantry (Consolidated), 2nd & 10th US Regular Infantry (Consolidated), 11th US Regular Infantry, 17th US Regular Infantry

3RD BRIGADE (Gouverneur Kemble Warren, Colonel): 5th New York Volunteers (Duryee's Zouaves), 10th New York Volunteers (National Zouaves)

Unattached formation: 1st US Volunteer Sharpshooters

ARTILLERY: E & G/1st US Regular Artillery, I/5th US Regular Artillery, K/5th US Regular Artillery

3RD DIVISION

Andrew Atkinson Humphreys, Brigadier General USV (Organized 12 Sept 1862, arrived on field as reinforcements 18 Sept 1862)

1ST BRIGADE (Erastus Barnard Tyler, Brigadier General USV): 91st Pennsylvania Volunteers, 126th Pennsylvania

Continued overleaf

ORDER OF BATTLE: UNITED STATES FORCES continued

Volunteers, 129th Pennsylvania Volunteers, 134th Pennsylvania Volunteers

2ND BRIGADE (Peter Allabach, Colonel 131st Pennsylvania Volunteers): 123rd Pennsylvania Volunteers, 131st Pennsylvania Volunteers, 133rd Pennsylvania Volunteers 155th Pennsylvania Volunteers

ARTILLERY: C/1st New York Volunteer Artillery, L/1st Ohio Volunteer Artillery

ARTILLERY RESERVE

K/1st US Regular Artillery, G/4th US Regular Artillery, 5th Independent Battery, New York Volunteer Light Artillery, A/1st New York Volunteer Artillery Battalion, B/1st New York Volunteer Artillery Battalion, C/1st New York Volunteer Artillery Battalion, D/1st New York Volunteer Artillery Battalion

VI CORPS

William Buel Franklin, Major General USV

Escort: B & G/6th Pennsylvania Volunteer Cavalry

1ST DIVISION

Henry Warner Slocum, Major General USV

1ST BRIGADE (Alfred Thomas Archimedes Torbert, Brigadier General USV): 1st New Jersey Volunteers, 2nd New Jersey Volunteers, 3rd New Jersey Volunteers, 4th New Jersey Volunteers

2ND BRIGADE (Joseph Jackson Bartlett, Colonel 27th New York Volunteers): 5th Maine Volunteers, 16th New York Volunteers, 27th New York Volunteers, 96th Pennsylvania Volunteers

3RD BRIGADE (John Newton, Brigadier General USV): 18th New York Volunteers, 31st New York Volunteers, 32nd New York Volunteers, 95th Pennsylvania Volunteers

ARTILLERY: D/2nd US Regular Artillery, 1st Independent Battery, Massachusetts Volunteer Light Artillery, 1st Independent Battery, New Jersey Volunteer Light Artillery, A/Maryland Volunteer Light Artillery

2ND DIVISION

William F. Smith, Major General USV

1ST BRIGADE (Winfield Scott Hancock, Brigadier General USV): 6th Maine Volunteers, 43rd New York Volunteers, 49th Pennsylvania Volunteers, 137th Pennsylvania Volunteers, 5th Wisconsin Volunteers

2ND BRIGADE (William Thomas Harbaugh Brooks, Brigadier General USV): 2nd Vermont Volunteers, 3rd Vermont Volunteers, 4th Vermont Volunteers, 5th Vermont Volunteers, 6th Vermont Volunteers

3RD BRIGADE (William Howard Irwin, Colonel 49th New York Volunteers): 7th Maine Volunteers, 20th New York Volunteers, 33rd New York Volunteers, 49th New York Volunteers, 77th New York Volunteers

ARTILLERY: F/5th US Regular Artillery, 1st Independent Battery, New York Volunteer Light Artillery, B/Maryland Volunteer Light Artillery

1ST DIVISION

Darius Nash Couch, Major General USV

(Attached to VI Corps as 3rd Division, remainder of IV Corps in the Department of Southern Virginia. 1st Division/IV Corps became formally 3rd Division/ VI Corps as of 26 Sept 1862.)

1ST BRIGADE (Charles Devens, Brigadier General USV): 7th Massachusetts Volunteers, 10th Massachusetts Volunteers, 36th New York Volunteers, 2nd Rhode Island Volunteers

2ND BRIGADE (Albion Parris Howe, Brigadier General USV): 62nd New York Volunteers (Anderson's Zouaves), 93rd Pennsylvania Volunteers, 98th Pennsylvania Volunteers, 102nd Pennsylvania Volunteers, 139th Pennsylvania Volunteers

3RD BRIGADE (John Cochrane, Brigadier General USV): 65th New York Volunteers, 67th New York Volunteers, 122nd New York Volunteers, 23rd Pennsylvania Volunteers, 61st Pennsylvania Volunteers, 82nd Pennsylvania Volunteers

ARTILLERY: G/2nd US Regular artillery, C/1st Pennsylvania Volunteer Artillery, D/1st Pennsylvania Volunteer Artillery, 3rd Independent Battery, New York Volunteer Light Artillery

IX CORPS

Ambrose Everett Burnside, Major General USV

Jesse Lee Reno, Major General USV

Jacob Dolson Cox, Brigadier General USV

(Burnside considered himself in command of the right wing of the Army of the Potomac, consisting of his own IX Corps and I Corps led by Hooker, a command he did exercise at South Mountain on 14 Sept. McClellan had, however, ended this arrangement upon the arrival of the army at the Antietam battlefield. This was a fact that Burnside was either unaware of, or of which he deliberately took no notice; the result being some command confusion on the Federal left during the engagement of Antietam Creek. General Reno had led IX Corps at South Mountain, while Burnside was exercising his wing command; and was killed in that engagement. General Burnside insisted at Antietam that General Cox, the leader of the attached Kanawha Division from West Virginia, who was senior to Burnside's other divisional commanders, was actually the leader of IX Corps.)

Escort: G/1st Maine Volunteer Cavalry

1ST DIVISION

Orlando Bolivar Willcox, Brigadier General USV

1ST BRIGADE (Benjamin Christ, Colonel 50th Pennsylvania Volunteers): 28th Massachusetts Volunteers, 17th Michigan Volunteers, 79th New York Volunteers, 50th Pennsylvania Volunteers

2ND BRIGADE (Thomas Welsh, Colonel): 8th Michigan Volunteers, 46th New York Volunteers, 45th Pennsylvania Volunteers, 100th Pennsylvania Volunteers

ARTILLERY: E/2nd US Regular Artillery, 8th Independent Battery, Massachusetts Volunteer Light Artillery

2ND DIVISION

Samuel Davis Sturgis, Brigadier General USV

1st Brigade (James Nagle, Brigadier

General USV): 2nd Maryland Volunteers, 6th New Hampshire Volunteer, 9th New Hampshire Volunteers, 48th Pennsylvania Volunteers

2ND BRIGADE (Edward Ferrero, Brigadier General USV): 21st Massachusetts Volunteers, 35th Massachusetts Volunteers, 51st New York Volunteers, 51st Pennsylvania Volunteers

ARTILLERY: E/4th US Regular Artillery, D/Pennsylvania Volunteer Light Artillery

---

3RD DIVISION

Isaac Peace Rodman, Brigadier General USV

1ST BRIGADE (Harrison Stiles Fairchild, Colonel 89th New York Volunteers): 9th New York Volunteers (Hawkin's Zouaves), 89th New York Volunteers, 103rd New York Volunteers

2ND BRIGADE (Edward Harland, Colonel 8th Connecticut Volunteers): 8th Connecticut Volunteers, 11th Connecticut Volunteers, 16th Connecticut Volunteers, 4th Rhode Island Volunteers

ARTILLERY: A/5th US Regular Artillery

THE KANAWHA DIVISION

Jacob Dolson Cox, Brigadier General USV

Hugh Boyle Ewing, Colonel 30th Ohio Volunteers

1ST BRIGADE (Hugh Boyle Ewing, Colonel 30th Ohio Volunteers, Eliakim Parker Scammon, Colonel 23rd Ohio Volunteers): 12th Ohio Volunteers, 23rd Ohio Volunteers, 30th Ohio Volunteers, 1st Independent Battery, Ohio Volunteer Light Artillery, Gilmore's Independent Company, Ohio Volunteer Cavalry, Harrison's Independent Company, Ohio Volunteer Cavalry

2ND BRIGADE (George Crook, Colonel 36th Ohio Volunteers): 11th Ohio Volunteers, 28th Ohio Volunteers, 36th Ohio Volunteers, Independent Battery, Kentucky Volunteer Light Artillery, Schambeck's Independent Company, Illinois Volunteer Cavalry (The Chicago Dragoons)

UNATTACHED FORMATIONS: 6th New York Volunteer Cavalry (8 Cos.), 3rd Independent Company, Ohio Volunteer Cavalry, L & M/3rd US Regular Artillery

---

XII CORPS

Joseph King Fenno Mansfield, Major General USV

Alpheus Starkey Williams, Brigadier General USV

(General Mansfield was mortally wounded very early in the action and was replaced, after some confusion, by General Williams.)

Escort: L/1st Michigan Volunteer Cavalry

1ST DIVISION

Alpheus Starkey Williams, Brigadier General USV

Samuel Wylie Crawford, Brigadier General USV

1ST BRIGADE (Samuel Wylie Crawford, Brigadier General USV, Joseph Farmer Knipe, Colonel 46th Pennsylvania Volunteers): 5th Connecticut Volunteers (detached at Frederick 15 Sept.), 10th Maine Volunteers, 28th New York Volunteers, 46th Pennsylvania Volunteers, 124th Pennsylvania Volunteers, 125th Pennsylvania Volunteers, 128th Pennsylvania Volunteers

3RD BRIGADE (George Henry Gordon, Brigadier General USV): 27th Indiana Volunteers, 2nd Massachusetts Volunteers, 13th New Jersey Volunteers, 107th New York Volunteers, 3rd Wisconsin Volunteers

---

2ND DIVISION

George Sears Greene, Brigadier General USV

1ST BRIGADE (Hector Tyndale, Lt. Colonel 28th Pennsylvania Volunteers): 5th Ohio Volunteers, 7th Ohio Volunteers, 29th Ohio Volunteers (detached 9 Sept.), 66th Ohio Volunteers, 28th Pennsylvania Volunteers

2ND BRIGADE (Henry Stainbrook, Colonel): 3rd Maryland Volunteers, 102nd New York Volunteers, 109th Pennsylvania Volunteers (detached 13 Sept.), 111th Pennsylvania Volunteers

3rd Brigade (William Goodrich, Colonel): 3rd Delaware Volunteers, 60th New York Volunteers, 78th New York Volunteers, Purnell Maryland Volunteer Legion

ARTILLERY BRIGADE (C.L. Best, Captain 4th US Regular Artillery): F/4th US Regular Artillery, 4th Independent Battery, Maine Volunteer Light Artillery 6th Independent Battery, Maine Volunteer Light Artillery, M/1st New York Volunteer Artillery, 10th Independent Battery, New York Volunteer Light Artillery, E/Pennsylvania Volunteer Light Artillery, F/Pennsylvania Volunteer Light Artillery

---

CAVALRY DIVISION

Alfred Pleasonton, Major General USV

1ST CAVALRY BRIGADE (Charles Whiting, Major): 5th US Regular Cavalry, 6th US Regular Cavalry

2ND CAVALRY BRIGADE (John Franklin Farnsworth, Colonel 8th Illinois Volunteer Cavalry): 8th Illinois Volunteer Cavalry, 3rd Indiana Volunteer Cavalry, 8th Pennsylvania Volunteer Cavalry, 1st Massachusetts Volunteer Cavalry

3RD CAVALRY BRIGADE (Richard Rush, Colonel 6th Pennsylvania Volunteer Cavalry): 4th Pennsylvania Volunteer Cavalry, 6th Pennsylvania Volunteer Cavalry (Rush's Lancers)

4TH CAVALRY BRIGADE (Andrew McReynolds, Colonel): 1st New York Volunteer Cavalry, 12th Pennsylvania Volunteer Cavalry

5TH CAVALRY BRIGADE (Benjamin Franklin Davis, Colonel 8th New York Volunteer Cavalry): 8th New York Volunteer Cavalry, 3rd Pennsylvania Volunteer Cavalry

ARTILLERY: A/2nd US Regular Artillery, B & L/2nd US Regular Artillery, M/2nd US Regular Artillery, C/3rd US Regular Artillery

Unattached formations: 1st Maine Volunteer Cavalry (detached at Frederick 13 Sept.), 15th Pennsylvania Volunteer Cavalry

(It should be noted that in addition to the forces commanded by McClellan in the field during the Antietam campaign, there was a large garrison in and around the city of Washington behind substantial fortifications. McClellan left Major General Nathaniel P. Banks in

ORDER OF BATTLE: UNITED STATES FORCES continued

command of these forces and the direct defence of the Federal Capital. Banks had some 73,000 troops comprising III Corps led by Maj. General Samuel Peter Heintzelman, XI Corps (late I Corps/ Army of Virginia) under Major General Franz Sigel, and the garrison formations of Washington (that would ultimately become XXII Corps as of 1 February 1863) commanded by Major General Silas Casey.)

FORMATIONS ADDED 30 SEPT 1862:

To I Corps: 24th Michigan Volunteers, 121st Pennsylvania Volunteers, 136th Pennsylvania Volunteers, 142nd Pennsylvania Volunteers
To II Corps: 19th Maine Volunteers
To VI Corps: 37th Massachusetts Volunteers, 15th New Jersey Volunteers, 21st New Jersey Volunteers, 23rd New Jersey Volunteers, 26th New Jersey Volunteers
To IX Corps: 21st Connecticut Volunteers, 10th New Hamshire Volunteers, 11th New Hampshire Volunteers, 7th Rhode Island Volunteers
To XII Corps: 20th Connecticut Volunteers, 123rd New York Volunteers, 137th New York Volunteers, 140th New York Volunteers, 145th New York Volunteers, 149th New York Volunteers

MIDDLE DEPARTMENT

(VIII Corps):
Major General John E. Wool

DEFENCES OF BALTIMORE:
Colonel William W. Morris
18th Connecticut Volunteers, 5th New York Volunteer Heavy Artillery (6 Companies), 8th New York Volunteer Heavy Artillery, 13th Pennsylvania Volunteer Cavalry, C/ Purnell Maryland Volunteer Cavalry, 17th Independent Indiana Volunteer Light Artillery, I/2nd US Artillery, L/5th US Artillery

COVERING FORCES, BALTIMORE:
Brigadier General William H. Emory
2nd Maryland Eastern Shore Volunteers, 38th Massachusetts Volunteers, 6th New York Volunteer Heavy Artillery, 110th New York Volunteers, 114th New York Volunteers, 116th New York Volunteers, 128th New York Volunteers, 150th New York Volunteers

DEFENCES OF ANNAPOLIS:
Colonel John F. Staunton
67th Pennsylvania Volunteers, 131st New York Volunteers, B/ Purnell Maryland Volunteer Cavalry

DEFENCES MARYLAND EASTERN SHORE:
Brigadier General H.H. Lockwood
1st Maryland Eastern Shore Volunteers, A/ Purnell Maryland Volunteer Cavalry
FORT DELAWARE (Major Henry S. Burton): 1 Bn, Pennsylvania Volunteer Marine and Fortification Artillery, Pennsylvania Independent Volunteer Heavy Artillery (4 Companies)

RELAY HOUSE (Colonel C.L.K. Sumwalt): 138th Pennsylvania Volunteers, B/2nd New York Volunteer Artillery Bn
WILMINGTON, DELAWARE: 4th Delaware Volunteers
ELLICOT'S MILLS, MARYLAND: 12th New Jersey Volunteers
MONOCACY, MARYLAND: 14th New Jersey Volunteers
ANNAPOLIS JUNCTION, MARYLAND: 109th New York Volunteers
LAUREL, MARYLAND: 141st New York Volunteers
YORK, PENNSYLVANIA: The Patapsco Guards, Maryland Volunteers
PARKTON, MARYLAND: 140th Pennsylvania Volunteers
COCKEYVILLE, MARYLAND: 148th Pennsylvania Volunteers

TRANSFERRED 19 SEPT 1862 FROM THE MIDDLE DEPARTMENT TO THE DEPARTMENT OF THE OHIO: 23rd Illinois Volunteers, 2nd Potomac Home Brigade, Maryland Volunteers, 106th New York Volunteers, 84th Ohio Volunteers, 86th Ohio Volunteers, 87th Pennsylvania Volunteers, 6th West Virginia Volunteers, 10th West Virginia Volunteers, 11th West Virginia Volunteers, 12th West Virginia Volunteers, 1st West Virginia Volunteer Cavalry (one company), L/1st Illinois Volunteer Light Artillery

ORDER OF BATTLE: CONFEDERATE FORCES

Army of Northern Virginia:
General Robert E. Lee

LONGSTREET'S CORPS:
Major General James Longstreet

MCLAW'S DIVISION:
Major General Lafayette McLaws
KERSHAW'S BRIGADE (Brigadier General Joseph Brevard Kershaw): 2nd South Carolina, 3rd South Carolina, 7th South Carolina, 8th South Carolina
BARKSDALE'S BRIGADE (Brigadier

General William Barksdale): 13th Mississippi, 17th Mississippi, 18th Mississippi, 21st Mississippi
SEMME'S BRIGADE (Brigadier General Paul J. Semmes): 10th Georgia, 53rd Georgia, 15th Virginia, 32nd Virginia
COBB'S BRIGADE (Brigadier General Howell Cobb): 16th Georgia, 24th Georgia, 15th North Carolina, Cobb's Georgia Legion
ARTILLERY (Major J.P. Hamilton): North Carolina Battery, Manley's Battery, Georgia Battery, the 'Pulaski' Artillery,

Read's Battery, Georgia Battery, the 'Troup' Artillery, Carlton's Battery, Virginia Battery, the 'Richmond Fayette' Artillery, Macon's Battery, Virginia Battery, 1st Company/ Richmond Howitzers, McCarthy's Battery

ANDERSON'S DIVISION:
Major General Richard Heron Anderson
WILCOX'S BRIGADE (Colonel Alfred Cuming): 8th Alabama, 9th Alabama,

ORDER OF BATTLE: CONFEDERATE FORCES continued

10th Alabama, 11th Alabama
ARMISTEAD'S BRIGADE (Brigadier General Lewis Addison Armistead): 9th Virginia, 14th Virginia, 38th Virginia, 53rd Virginia, 57th Virginia
MAHONE'S BRIGADE (Colonel William A. Parham): 6th Virginia, 12th Virginia, 16th Virginia, 41st Virginia, 61st Virginia
FEATHERSTON'S BRIGADE (Brigadier General Winfield Scott Featherston): 12th Mississippi, 16th Mississippi, 19th Mississippi, 2nd Mississippi Battalion
PRYOR'S BRIGADE (Brigadier General Roger Atkinson Pryor): 14th Alabama, 2nd Florida, 5th Florida, 8th Florida, 3rd Virginia
WRIGHT'S BRIGADE (Brigadier General Ambrose Ransom Wright): 44th Alabama, 3rd Georgia, 22nd Georgia, 48th Georgia
ARTILLERY (Major John S. Saunders): Louisiana Battery, the 'Donaldson' Artillery, Maurin's Battery, Virginia Battery, Huger's Battery, Virginia Battery, Moorman's Battery, Virginia Battery, Thompson's or Grimes' Battery

JONES'S DIVISION:
Brigadier General David Rumph Jones
TOOMBS'S BRIGADE (Brigadier General Robert Toombs): 2nd Georgia, 15th Georgia, 17th Georgia, 20th Georgia
DRAYTON'S BRIGADE (Brigadier General Thomas Fenwick Drayton): 50th Georgia, 51st Georgia, 15th South Carolina, 3rd South Carolina Battalion
PICKETT'S BRIGADE (Colonel Eppa Hunton): 8th Virginia, 18th Virginia, 19th Virginia, 28th Virginia, 56th Virginia
KEMPER'S BRIGADE (Brigadier General James Lawson Kemper): 1st Virginia, 7th Virginia, 11th Virginia, 17th Virginia, 24th Virginia
JENKINS'S BRIGADE (Colonel Joseph Walker): 1st South Carolina, 2nd South Carolina (Rifles), 5th South Carolina, 6th South Carolina, 4th South Carolina Battalion, Palmetto South Carolina Sharpshooter Battalion
ANDERSON'S BRIGADE (Colonel George Thomas Anderson): 1st Georgia (1st Regulars), 7th Georgia, 8th Georgia, 9th Georgia, 11th Georgia
ARTILLERY: Virginia Battery, the 'Wise' Artillery, Brown's Battery, Virginia Battery, the 'Fauquier' Artillery, Stribling's Battery*, Virginia Battery,

the 'Loudoun' Artillery, Rogers' Battery*, Virginia Battery, the 'Turner' Artillery, Leake's Battery*
(*Not on the field at Antietam, remaining at Leesburg, Virginia.)

WALKER'S DIVISION:
Brigadier General John G. Walker
WALKER'S BRIGADE (Colonel Van H. Manning): 3rd Arkansas, 27th North Carolina, 46th North Carolina, 48th North Carolina, 30th Virginia, Virginia Battery, French's Battery
RANSOM'S BRIGADE (Brigadier General Robert Ransom): 24th North Carolina, 25th North Carolina, 35th North Carolina, 49th North Carolina, Virginia Battery, Branch's Battery

HOOD'S DIVISION:
Brigadier General John Bell Hood
HOOD'S BRIGADE (Colonel William Tatum Wofford): 18th Georgia, 1st Texas, 4th Texas, 5th Texas, Hampton's South Carolina Legion
LAW'S BRIGADE (Colonel Evander McIvor Law): 4th Alabama, 2nd Mississippi, 11th Mississippi, 6th North Carolina
ARTILLERY (Major B.W. Frobel): South Carolina Battery, the 'German' Artillery, Bachman's Battery, South Carolina Battery, the 'Palmetto' Artillery, Gordon's Battery, North Carolina Battery, the 'Rowan' Artillery, Reilly's Battery

EVAN'S SEPARATE BRIGADE (Brigadier General Nathan George Evans): 17th South Carolina, 18th South Carolina, 22nd South Carolina, 23rd South Carolina, The Holcombe South Carolina Legion, South Carolina Battery, the 'Macbeth' Artillery, Boyce's Battery

ARTILLERY RESERVE
The Washington Artillery (Colonel James B. Walton): Louisiana Battery, 1st Company 'Washington' Artillery, Squire's Battery, Louisiana Battery, 1nd Company 'Washington' Artillery, Richardson's Battery, Louisiana Battery, 3rd Company 'Washington' Artillery, Miller's Battery, Louisiana Battery, 4th Company 'Washington' Artillery, Eshleman's Battery
Lee's Reserve Artillery Battalion (Colonel Stephen Dill Lee): Virginia

Battery, the 'Ashland' Artillery, Woolfolk's Battery, Virginia Battery, the 'Bedford' Artillery, Jordan's Battery, Virginia Battery, Eubank's Battery, Virginia Battery, Parker's Battery, Louisiana Battery, the 'Madison' Artillery, Moody's Battery, South Carolina Battery, Elliot's Light Artillery, Brook's Battery

JACKSON'S CORPS:
Major General Thomas J. Jackson

EWELL'S DIVISION:
Brigadier General Alexander Robert Lawton
LAWTON'S BRIGADE (Colonel M. Douglas): 13th Georgia, 26th Georgia, 31st Georgia, 38th Georgia, 60th Georgia, 61st Georgia
TRIMBLE'S BRIGADE (Colonel James A. Walker): 15th Alabama, 12th Georgia, 21st Georgia, 21st North Carolina, 1st North Carolina Battalion
EARLY'S BRIGADE (Brigadier General Jubal Anderson Early): 13th Virginia, 25th Virginia, 31st Virginia, 44th Virginia, 49th Virginia, 52nd Virginia, 58th Virginia
HAYS' BRIGADE (Brigadier General Harry Thompson Hays): 5th Louisiana, 6th Louisiana, 7th Louisiana, 8th Louisiana, 14th Louisiana
ARTILLERY (Major A. R. Courtney): Virginia Battery, the 'Charlottesville' Artillery, Carrington's Battery, Virginia Battery, Johnson's Battery, Louisiana Battery, the 'Louisiana Guard' Artillery, D'Aquin's Battery, Virginia Battery, the 'Stauton' Artillery, Balthis' Battery*, Virginia Battery, the 'Courtney' Artillery, Latimer's Battery*, Maryland Battery, the 'Chesapeake' Artillery, Brown's Battery*, Maryland Battery, the 1st 'Maryland' Battery, Dement's Battery*
(*Not present at Antietam; remained at Shepherdstown, Maryland & at Harper's Ferry, Virginia.)

A. P. HILL'S DIVISION:
Major General Ambrose Powell Hill
BRANCH'S BRIGADE (Brigadier General Lawrence O'Bryon Branch): 7th North Carolina, 18th North Carolina, 28th North Carolina, 33rd North Carolina, 37th North Carolina

Continued overleaf

ORDER OF BATTLE: CONFEDERATE FORCES continued

ARCHER'S BRIGADE (Brigadier General James Jay Archer): 5th Alabama Battalion, 19th Georgia, 1st Tennessee, 7th Tennessee, 14th Tennessee
GREGG'S BRIGADE (Brigadier General Maxey Gregg):1st South Carolina (Provisional Army), 1st South Carolina (Rifles), 12th South Carolina, 13th South Carolina, 14th South Carolina
PENDER'S BRIGADE (Brigadier General William Dorsey Pender): 16th North Carolina, 22nd North Carolina, 34th North Carolina, 38th North Carolina
THOMAS'S BRIGADE (Colonel Edward Lloyd Thomas): 14th Georgia, 35th Georgia, 45th Georgia, 49th Georgia
FIELD'S BRIGADE (Colonel Brockenbrough): 40th Virginia, 47th Virginia, 55th Virginia, 22nd Virginia Battalion
ARTILLERY: Virginia Battery, Crenshaw's Battery, Virginia Battery, the 'Fredericksburg' Artillery, Braxton's Battery, Virginia Battery, the 'Purcell' Artillery, Pegram's Battery, Virginia Battery, the 'Letcher' Artillery, Davidson's Battery*, Virginia Battery, the 'Middlesex' Artillery, Fleet's Battery**, North Carolina Battery, Latham's Battery (Branch's)**, South Carolina Battery, the 'Pee Dee' Artillery, McIntosh's Battery
(*Not present at Antietam; remained at Harper's Ferry. **Not present at Antietam; remained at Leesburg.)

JACKSON'S DIVISION:

Brigadier General John Robert Jones
WINDER'S BRIGADE: THE 'STONEWALL' BRIGADE (Colonel A.J. Grigsby): 2nd Virginia, 4th Virginia, 5th Virginia, 27th Virginia, 33rd Virginia
TALIAFERRO'S BRIGADE (Colonel E. T. H. Warren): 47th Alabama, 48th Alabama, 10th Virginia, 23rd Virginia, 37th Virginia
JONES'S BRIGADE (Colonel Bradley Tyler Johnson): 21st Virginia, 42nd Virginia, 48th Virginia, 1st Virginia Battalion (the 'Irish' Battalion)
STARKE'S BRIGADE (Brigadier General William E. Starke): 1st Louisiana, 2nd Louisiana, 9th Louisiana, 10th Louisiana, 15th Louisiana, Coppen's Louisiana Zouave Battalion
ARTILLERY (Major L.M. Shumaker): Virginia Battery, the 'Allegheny' Artillery, Carpenter's Battery, Virginia Battery, the 'Danville' Artillery,

Wooding's Battery, Virginia Battery, the 'Lee' Artillery, Raines' Battery, Virginia Battery, the 'Hampden' Artillery, Caskie's Battery, Virginia Battery, the 1st 'Rockbridge' Artillery, Poague's Battery, Maryland Battery, Brockenbrough's Battery

D. H. HILL'S DIVISION:

Major General Daniel Harvey Hill
RIPLEY'S BRIGADE (Brigadier General Roswell Sabine Ripley): 4th Georgia, 44th Georgia, 1st North Carolina, 3rd North Carolina
GARLAND'S BRIGADE (Brigadier General Samuel Garland [KIA.South Mountain] Colonel D. K. MacRae): 5th North Carolina, 12th North Carolina, 13th North Carolina, 20th North Carolina, 23rd North Carolina
RODES'S BRIGADE (Brigadier General Robert Emmet Rodes): 3rd Alabama, 5th Alabama, 6th Alabama, 12th alabama, 26th Alabama
ANDERSON'S BRIGADE (Brigadier General George Burgwyn Anderson): 2nd North Carolina, 4th North Carolina, 14th North Carolina, 30th North Carolina
COLQUITT'S BRIGADE (Colonel Alfred Holt Colquitt): 13th Alabama, 6th Georgia, 23rd Georgia, 27th Georgia, 28th Georgia
ARTILLERY (Major Pierson): Alabama Battery, Hardaway's Battery, Alabama Battery, the 'Jeff Davis' Artillery, Bondurant's Battery, Virginia Battery, Jones's Battery, Virginia Battery, the 'King William' Artillery, Carter's Battery

ARTILLERY RESERVE

Brigadier General William Nelson Pendleton
BROWN'S RESERVE ARTILLERY BATTALION (Colonel J. Thompson Brown): Virginia Battery, the 'Powhatan' Artillery, Dance's Battery, Virginia Battery, 2nd Company Richmond Howitzers, Watson's Battery, Virginia Battery, 3rd Company Richmond Howitzers, Smith's Battery, Virginia Battery, the 'Salem' Artillery, Hupp's Battery, Virginia Battery, the 'Williamsburg' Artillery, Coke's Battery
JONES'S RESERVE ARTILLERY BATTALION* (Major H. P. Jones): Virginia Battery, the 'Morris' Artillery, Page's Battery, Virginia Battery, the 'Orange' Artillery,

Peyton's Battery, Virginia Battery, Wimbish's Battery, Virginia Battery, Turner's Battery
(*Assigned to D. H. Hill's Division.)
CUTT'S RESERVE ARTILLERY BATTALION* (Lt Colonel A. S. Cutts): Georgia Battery, Blackshear's Battery, Georgia Battery, the 'Irwin' Artillery, Lane's Battery, Georgia Battery, Patterson's Battery, Georgia Battery, Ross's Battery, North Carolina Battery, Lloyd's Battery
NELSON'S RESERVE ARTILLERY BATTALION (Major William Nelson): Virginia Battery, the 'Amherst' Artillery, Kirkpatrick's Battery, Virginia Battery, the 'Fluvanna' Artillery, Ancell's Battery, Virginia Battery, Huckstep's Battery, Virginia Battery, Johnson's Battery, Georgia Battery, Milledge's Battery
UNATTACHED BATTERIES: Virginia Battery, Cutshaw's Battery, Virginia Battery, the 'Dixie' Artillery, Chapman's Battery, Virginia Battery, the 'Magruder' Artillery, Page's Battery, Virginia Battery, the 'New Market' Artillery, Rice's Battery, Virginia Battery, the 'Thomas' Artillery, Anderson's Battery**
(*Assigned to D.H. Hill's Division. **Not present at Antietam, remaining at Leesburg.)

CAVALRY DIVISION:

Major General James Ewell Brown Stuart
LEE'S CAVALRY BRIGADE (Brigadier General Fitzhugh Lee): 1st Virginia Cavalry, 3rd Virginia Cavalry, 4th Virginia Cavalry, 5th Virginia Cavalry, 9th Virginia Cavalry
ROBERTSON'S CAVALRY BRIGADE (Brigadier General Beverly Holcombe Robertson): 2nd Virginia Cavalry, 6th Virginia Cavalry, 7th Virginia Cavalry, 12th Virginia Cavalry, 17th Virginia Cavalry Battalion
HAMPTON'S CAVALRY BRIGADE (Brigadier General Wade Hampton): 1st North Carolina Cavalry, 2nd South Carolina Cavalry, 10th Virginia Cavalry, Cobb's Georgia Cavalry Legion, The 'Jeff Davis' Alabama-Mississippi Cavalry Legion
HORSE ARTILLERY (Captain John Pelham): Virginia Battery, Pelham's Battery, Virginia Battery, Chew's Battery, South Carolina Battery, Hart's Battery

SOUTH MOUNTAIN

'I feel as reasonably confident of success', wrote McClellan to his wife on the morning of 14 September, 'as any one well can who trusts in a higher power.' McClellan intended to take advantage of the knowledge he had gained of the division of Lee's army through the capture of Special Order 191. He ordered Major General William Franklin's VI Corps to take Crampton's Gap, with the additional mission of offering relief to the Federal garrison at Harper's Ferry. The main Federal effort would be made twelve miles north by IX Corps led against Fox's Gap by Major General Jesse Reno, and I Corps led by Major General Joseph Hooker against Turner's Gap. The operation was directed by the commander of the right wing, Major General Ambrose Burnside. The intention was to force the passes, move on Boonsboro, and separate Longstreet from Jackson. The remainder of the Federal army would support Burnside's endeavours.

The Battle of Crampton's Gap

Major General Franklin arrived with VI Corps at Burkittsville, on the road south of Crampton's Gap, at noon. The pass was defended by elements of Mahone's Virginia brigade of Richard Anderson's division, led by Colonel William Parham, and elements of Robertson's cavalry brigade. The whole Confederate force was commanded by Thomas Munford, Colonel of the 2nd Virginia Cavalry of Robertson's brigade. Thomas Taylor Munford (1831–1918) had been a member of the 1852 graduating class of the Virginia Military Institute, and a farmer before the War. He was now an experienced combat leader, attempting with elements of two Confederate brigades to defend a mountain pass against a Federal force of two divisions. Munford placed the field pieces of Chew's Virginia Battery half-way up the mountain, to the west of the road.

▶ *A mountain range separated Lee's divided army from McClellan's united one. The only way over the range was through a series of passes, known locally as 'gaps'. This one is Turner's Gap, looking south-east. Rhode was positioned on the hill that slopes to the left, while Gibbon's men were down in the hollow. Generals Reno and Garland were killed on the mountain to the south, on the right, Wise's Field at Fox's Gap.*

Crampton's Gap, 14 September 1862

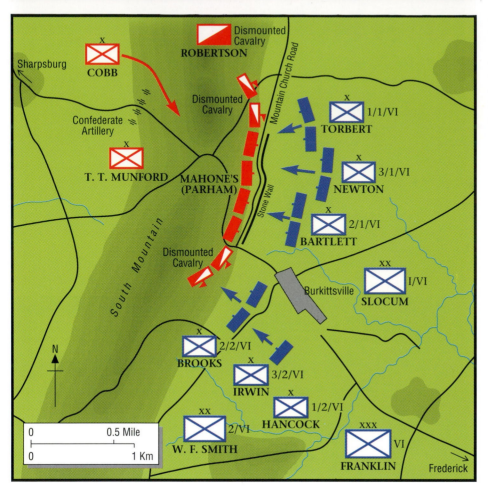

Dismounted Cavalry
ROBERTSON
COBB
Sharpsburg
Dismounted Cavalry
Confederate Artillery
Mountain Church Road
T. T. MUNFORD
MAHONE'S (PARHAM)
Stone Wall
1/1/VI
TORBERT
3/1/VI
NEWTON
2/1/VI
BARTLETT
Dismounted Cavalry
South Mountain
Burkittsville
I/VI
SLOCUM
N
2/2/VI
BROOKS
3/2/VI
IRWIN
1/2/VI
HANCOCK
2/VI
W. F. SMITH
VI
FRANKLIN
Frederick

0   0.5 Mile
0   1 Km

▶ *Major General William B. Franklin commanded VI Corps at Antietam, leading his troops through Crampton's Gap at South Mountain. The sash and elaborate epaulettes, shown in this period print, would have not been worn in the field.*

He placed the 6th and 12th Virginia Regiments under Colonel Parham along a stone wall, near the base of the mountain, to the east of the road. Parham's flanks were covered by the 2nd and 12th Virginia Cavalry Regiments deployed as dismounted skirmishers. Munford would hold this position against superior forces for nearly three hours.

Franklin placed the 1st Division/VI Corps led by Major General Henry W. Slocum to the right, or east side of the road, and ordered it to move against the Confederate centre and left. Slocum did so, supported by Captain Wolcott's Battery A/Maryland (Federal), Light Artillery. Slocum advanced with Colonel Joseph Bartlett's 2nd Brigade/1st Division on the left, nearest the road, and Brigadier General Alfred Torbert's 1st Brigade/1st Division on the extreme Federal right. Brigadier General John

Newton's 3rd Brigade/1st Division constituted the reserve.

The advance was initiated by the 2nd Brigade, led by Joseph Jackson Bartlett (1834-1893), a lawyer before the War, and now Colonel of the 27th New York Volunteers. Bartlett led his New Yorkers and the other regiments of his brigade against the stone wall held by Parham's Virginians through 'a well directed fire' from Chew's field pieces up the slope of the mountain. Captain Romeyn Beck Ayres (1825–88) meanwhile directed the guns of his Battery F/5th United States Artillery in a counter-battery duel with Chew's cannon in an attempt to cover the Federal advance. Ayres was an 1847 graduate of the United States Military Academy, a veteran of the war with Mexico, and one of the few regulars sprinkled among the Federal volunteer

army. Major General William F. Smith's 2nd Division/VI Corps conformed to Slocom's advance by moving forward on the left or western side of the road, with Colonel William Irwin's 3rd Brigade/2nd Division on Smith's right nearest the road, and Brigadier General William Brook's 2nd Brigade/2nd Division on the extreme Federal left. Brigadier General Winfield Scott Hancock's 1st Brigade/2nd Division constituted Smith's reserve.

Colonel Bartlett encountered stiff resistance and was ultimately reinforced from Newton's brigade. The final Federal movement was a general advance sometime around 1430. 'The men swept forward, with a cheer', Franklin wrote in his report, 'over the stone wall, dislodging the enemy, and pursuing him over the mountain side to the crest of the hill and down the opposite slope.' VI Corps claimed the capture of 400 prisoners from seventeen different organizations, three colours, a field piece, and 700 discarded weapons. Franklin stated that his men buried 150 Confederate soldiers on the field.

Colonel Munford reported minimal losses in his cavalry regiments, but admitted to heavier casualties among the infantry, stating in his report, 'Colonel Parham's loss must have been heavy, as they were a long time engaged, and the firing was as heavy as I ever heard.' The Confederate force commanded by Colonel Munford had, nonetheless, accomplished its mission. Franklin made no further significant advance that day beyond Crampton's Gap, discouraged by the arrival of Brigadier General Howell Cobb's brigade, and other elements of McLaws' Confederate Division in his front. Meanwhile, the Federal garrison commander at Harper's Ferry was forced to surrender 12,000 men and a considerable amount of war material at 0800 the following morning, 15 September, to Major General Thomas Jackson's Confederate forces.

The Battle of Turner's Gap

While Franklin was fighting his battle at Crampton's Gap, the main Federal effort was being made against the Turner's Gap position by the Federal right wing led by Major General Burnside. Major General James Longstreet was at Hagerstown, Maryland, with two Confederate divisions, while Major General Jackson was attempting to take Harper's Ferry with the majority of Lee's forces. That left the Confederate division of Daniel Harvey Hill, at Boonsboro on the evening of 13 September, to defend the Turner's Gap position. It was a critical mission because if the Federal Army of the Potomac swept Hill aside and interposed itself between Longstreet and Jackson, then Lee's Army of Northern Virginia would be beaten in detail, if not annihilated. Corporal Woodford of the 16th Connecticut Volunteers in the Federal IX Corps wrote, 'A good many of the old soldiers think that the next battle will decide the contest. I hope so, but I have my doubts about it.'

Hill sent Garland's brigade to hold the lower Fox's Gap, and Colonel Alfred Colquitt's brigade into Turner's Gap proper. He retained his other three brigades (G. B. Anderson, Rodes, and Ripley) near Boonsboro until the situation became clear.

The North Carolinian regiments sent to defend Fox's Gap were commanded by Brigadier General Samuel Garland, an 1849 graduate of the Virginia

Military Institute. Garland had received a law degree from the University of Virginia and practised law in his home town of Lynchburg, Virginia. Garland was from a prominent family, and was much respected in his community. He had raised a volunteer company as early as 1859, following the arrest of John Brown. Garland was observed on the morning of 14 September walking behind his men, inspecting his positions in Fox's Gap, and deep in a discussion of classical literature with the officers accompanying him.

The leading formation of Federal IX Corps approaching Garland's position was the Kanawha Division, recently attached to the IX Corps from operations in West Virginia, commanded by Brigadier General Jacob Cox. Jacob Dolson Cox (1828–1900) was a lawyer and prominent Republican abolitionist before the War. He would develop into one of the better 'citizen soldiers' the War produced, even though he had no formal military training. Cox was an authority, interestingly enough, on European cathedral architecture. He

placed his 1st Brigade led by Colonel Eliakim Scammon on his left and his 2nd Brigade commanded by Colonel George Crook on his right, and advanced at 0900 through cultivated fields and up a steep slope against Garland's waiting rebel infantry.

Cox detached the 23rd Ohio Volunteers from his main body, and sent it on a wide flanking movement to his extreme left, in order to gain a position behind the Confederate right. The 23rd Ohio was commanded by a future president of the USA. Lieutenant Colonel Rutherford B. Hays, who would be elected President of the United States after the disputed election of 1876 was decided by congressional committee and the famous 'Compromise of 1877'. The manner of the Republican victory in 1876 earned Hays the nicknames 'Old eight to seven', the vote in the committee that awarded the

▼ *Federal artillery takes position under fire at South Mountain as the Confederate forces seek to delay McClellan's advance and make time for Lee's army to concentrate.*

Republicans the disputed electoral votes, and 'His fraudulence'. Hays would serve as president from 1877 to 1881, but that was in the future, and now he managed to get his men in position unobserved by Garland's Southerners. Cox advanced his brigades against Garland's line, supported by artillery fire from the 10- and 20-pounder Parrott rifles of McMullin's Ohio and Simmond's Kentucky batteries. 'The rebels stood firmly, and kept up a murderous fire', wrote Cox in his report on the action, 'until the advancing line was within a few feet of them, when they broke and fled over the crest into the shelter of a dense thicket skirting the other side.' The Confederate infantry tried several times to dislodge Hays' 23rd Ohio and to retake the crest. Brigadier General Samuel Sturgis's 2nd Division/IX Corps arrived on Cox's right, and the Southern general Garland was killed in the fighting. The Southerners in Fox's Gap streamed towards the rear. It was noon.

The remainder of the IX Corps arrived on the battlefield. The 1st Division led by Brigadier General Orlando Willcox took position on Sturgis's right, and the 3rd Division commanded by Brigadier General Isaac Rodman moved into place on the right of Willcox. The commander of the right wing and the official commander of IX Corps, Major General Ambrose Burnside also had arrived on the field. Burnside was uncertain of Confederate

▲ *Reno approached from the Middletown valley and the Catoctin range on the left towards Fox's Gap. The old Sharpsburg road lies between the stone wall and the rail fence seen here.*

strength in the area, and he therefore halted further operations until Federal I Corps got into position on the right of IX Corps. The result was a lull in the fighting of some two hours' duration.

It was time put to good use by the desperate Daniel Harvey Hill, for had Cox continued the advance it is extremely doubtful if the Southern forces could have prevented the capture of Turner's Gap by early afternoon. There would have been ample time for the Federals to continue the forward movement and place themselves between Longstreet and Jackson. 'Providentially, they were ignorant of their success,' wrote Hill in his report on South Mountain. He sent G. B. Anderson's, Ripley's, and Drayton's brigades (the latter an element of D. R. Jones's division of Longstreet's command) down the road towards where Garland's Brigade had been posted to make contact with Colonel Thomas Lafayette Rosser's 5th Virginia Cavalry, which had been operating beyond Garland's right rear. Hill retained Colquitt's brigade astride the main road in the gap proper and dispatched the Alabamian Brigade of Brigadier General Robert Rodes to the extreme Confederate left flank.

Turner's Gap and Fox's Gap: The Battle of South Mountain, morning to about 1400, 14 Sept 1862

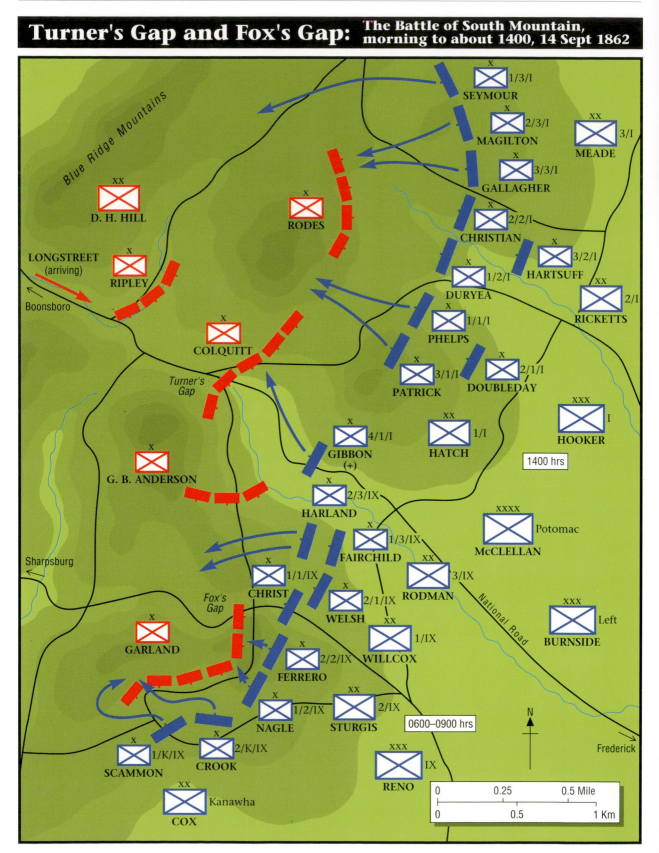

Blue Ridge Mountains

D. H. HILL ^{XX}

LONGSTREET (arriving)

RIPLEY ^{X}

Boonsboro

RODES ^{X}

SEYMOUR ^{X} 1/3/I

MAGILTON ^{X} 2/3/I

MEADE ^{XX} 3/I

GALLAGHER ^{X} 3/3/I

CHRISTIAN ^{X} 2/2/I

HARTSUFF ^{X} 3/2/I

RICKETTS ^{XX} 2/I

DURYEA ^{X} 1/2/I

PHELPS ^{X} 1/1/I

PATRICK ^{X} 3/1/I

DOUBLEDAY ^{X} 2/1/I

COLQUITT ^{X}

Turner's Gap

G. B. ANDERSON ^{X}

GIBBON ^{X} 4/1/I (+)

HATCH ^{XX} 1/I

HOOKER ^{XXX} I

1400 hrs

HARLAND ^{X} 2/3/IX

FAIRCHILD ^{X} 1/3/IX

McCLELLAN ^{XXXX} Potomac

Sharpsburg

CHRIST ^{X} 1/1/IX

Fox's Gap

GARLAND ^{X}

WELSH ^{X} 2/1/IX

RODMAN ^{XX} 3/IX

National Road

WILLCOX ^{XX} 1/IX

BURNSIDE ^{XXX} Left

FERRERO ^{X} 2/2/IX

N

NAGLE ^{X} 1/2/IX

STURGIS ^{XX} 2/IX

0600–0900 hrs

Frederick

SCAMMON ^{X} 1/K/IX

CROOK ^{X} 2/K/IX

RENO ^{XXX} IX

COX ^{XX} Kanawha

| 0 | 0.25 | 0.5 Mile |
| 0 | 0.5 | 1 Km |

The leading element of Federal I Corps, its 3rd Division, led by Brigadier General George Meade, began arriving on the battlefield after 1330. Meade was ordered to make a diversion in favour of a continued advance of IX Corps by striking the extreme left flank of the Confederate position. George Gordon Meade (1815–72) was an 1835 graduate of the United States Military Academy, a pre-war engineer and professional soldier. He would end the American Civil War commanding the Federal Army of the Potomac. Meade was known to have a terrible temper, and his subordinates unkindly suggested that his disposition might be compared to 'an old snapping turtle'. The division commanded by Meade at South Mountain constituted the 'Pennsylvania Reserves', thirteen infantry regiments from Pennsylvania grouped into what had become one of the hardest hitting formations in the Army of the Potomac. Pennsylvania had received far more men volunteering to support the Federal Union in 1861 than the national government had expected, and rather than turn away these enthusiastic men Governor Curtin of Pennsylvania had organized and equipped them at state expense. Meade's regiments had long ago received Federal designations, but they insisted on still being known as the 'Pennsylvania

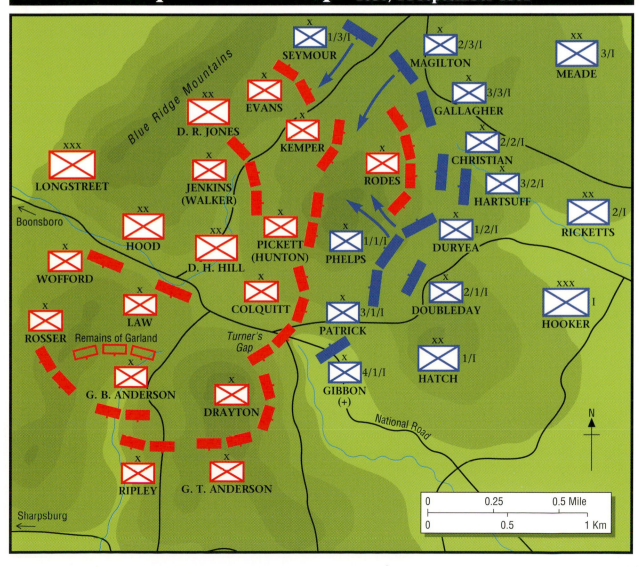

Turner's Gap and Fox's Gap: The Battle of South Mountain, 1630, 14 September 1862

Reserves'. State pride was as important to Northern men as it was to their opponents. The 13th Pennsylvania Reserves were, for example, actually the 42nd Pennsylvania Volunteers, but the men of Colonel McNeil's 'Bucktail' regiment would have insisted to all ill-informed strangers that they were part of the 'Pennsylvania Reserves' Division equipped by the State of Pennsylvania. Colonel McNeil's regiment led the advance of Meade's division against the Confederate left, now held by Robert Rodes's Alabamians, shortly after 1400. Meade made contact and deployed his division. He ordered Brigadier General Truman Seymour's 1st Brigade with the 13th Pennsylvania Reserves in the advance to swing around the Confederate left; Colonel Albert Magilton was told to lead his 2nd Brigade down the road against the Confederate left, and Colonel Thomas Gallagher was instructed to assault the centre of the Confederate line.

Rodes faced heavy odds at South Mountain on 14 September, as Meade's Pennsylvanians advanced against his Alabamians. He stood his ground. 'Rodes handled his little brigade in a most admirable and gallant manner', wrote D. H. Hill in his report on the action, 'fighting for hours vastly superior odds.' Hill finally began to receive reinforcements from Longstreet starting at 1500, and an hour later the Confederate position was more secure as Brigadier General John Bell Hood's two-brigade division supported the line formed facing Fox's Gap by (from the Confederate right) the cavalry of Rosser and the brigades of G. B. Anderson (supported by the remains of Garland's Brigade), Ripley, G. T. Anderson, and Drayton. (G. T. Anderson's and Drayton's brigades belonged to D. R. Jones's division of Longstreet's command, and the remainder were a part of D. H. Hill's division.) Colquitt's Brigade of Hill's division still held the crossroads, and Hill's other formation, Rodes' Brigade, stubbornly resisted Meade's advance. Brigadier General David Jones led his other brigades, Pickett's Virginians under Colonel Eppa Hunton, Jenkins' South Carolinians under Colonel Joseph Walker, Kemper's Virginians, and Evans's separate South Carolina Brigade to Rodes' support. It was after 1600.

The remainder of Federal I Corps began arriving on the field. The 1st Division led by the 1st Brigade commander Brigadier General John Hatch went forward against the gap between Rodes' right flank and the left flank of Colquitt's brigade, making some progress. The hole in the Confederate line was plugged by the arrival of Jones's brigades. The 2nd Division/I Corps directed by Brigadier General James Ricketts took position between the divisions commanded by Hatch and Meade. Colonel John Gibbon took the 4th Brigade/1st Division/I Corps, the 'Iron Brigade' (19th Indiana, 2nd Wisconsin, 6th Wisconsin, and 7th Wisconsin), up the road against Colonel Colquitt's Georgian regiments.

The engagement dragged on past nightfall, as Ricketts wrote in his report, 'over very rough ground'. Major General Jesse L. Reno, commanding the Federal IX Corps was killed after dark while reconnoitring his front. The battle finally came to a conclusion. 'It being very dark, our troops were directed to remain in position', wrote Major General Hooker, commanding Federal I Corps, and 'to sleep on their arms.' The Confederates departed the field that night. By noon on 15 September, the

▶ *Major General Jesse L. Reno (above right) was mortally wounded while leading his division into Fox's Gap at South Mountain. He actually fell near the stump in the middle of the field beyond the wall (right), while men fought for the wooded crest on the left of the field. The house is the Wise home.*

Federal Army was in sole possession of Turner's and Fox's Gaps. It had been a Federal tactical victory, as Crampton's, Turner's, and Fox's Gaps over the South Mountain range of the Blue Ridge Mountains had been cleared of Confederate troops. The various Southern commands under Munford and Hill had, however, purchased a strategic victory. The Army of the Potomac had not succeeded in dividing the Army of Northern Virginia. McClellan had moved upon the capture of Special Order 191, but not swiftly enough.

On 13 September, when he learned that Special Order 191 was in Federal hands Lee had ordered a withdrawal south of the Potomac River. Now, early on 15 September, Lee was informed that Jackson had taken Harper's Ferry with its large Federal garrison. In addition, Hill had managed to hold Turner's and Fox's Gaps for the entire day on 14 September, and Federal VI Corps had not advanced much beyond Crampton's Gap. Lee rescinded the withdrawal order. He ordered his divisions to concentrate on Sharpsburg, Maryland, where he would offer battle along the Antietam Creek.

OPPOSING PLANS, 17 SEPTEMBER 1862

General Lee has been criticized by historians for making the decision of accepting battle in Maryland following the engagements at South Mountain and Crampton's Gap. He had averted the potential for complete disaster created by the capture of Special Order 191 on 13 September, and Jackson had managed to take Harper's Ferry. But if Lee should fight and lose, the Potomac River to the Confederate rear represented a substantial military obstacle to a retreating army. In addition, the Southerners were outnumbered and the Federals seemed to have the advantage of momentum as a result of the battles for the mountain gaps. The cautious course for the Army of Northern Virginia might have been to accept the Harper's Ferry success, be grateful that the Federals had not been able to take full advantage of Special Order 191, and return to Virginia with the army intact. Robert E. Lee was, however, as Longstreet once remarked 'the most combative man in the army', and there were other considerations.

Lee may have suspected that McClellan's customary battlefield caution would reassert itself; moreover, large numbers of Marylanders had not come to join the Southern army. The engagements at South Mountain and at Crampton's Gap, however successful for the South from a strategic viewpoint, might very well be construed as tactical defeats. The South needed battlefield success in Maryland to encourage Southern sympathies and to impress foreign capitals. Lee may have believed that he could not return to Virginia for political reasons without an engagement that could be reasonably presented as a Southern success. Tactically, Lee prepared a defensive position in such a manner as to allow reaction to Federal advances as circumstances dictated.

McClellan did not follow the Confederate army from the South Mountain battlefield on 15 September with sufficient vigour. Lee was able to complete the concentration of his army at Sharpsburg by the afternoon of 16 September (with the exception of A. P. Hill's division still processing the men and material captured at Harper's Ferry) without any real interference from the Northern army. There was some skirmishing around the Sharpsburg positions on 16 September, but nothing really serious developed. McClellan contented himself that day with reconnoitring the enemy positions and formulating his battle plan.

The general battle plan developed by McClellan on 16 September is a matter of some speculation. The available evidence and the events of the engagement would suggest that he envisaged an *echelon* assault starting on the Federal right with Hooker's I Corps, followed by Mansfield's XII Corps, followed by Sumner's II Corps, moving from the Confederate left towards the Confederate centre. The basic concept of an *echelon* assault was that pressure be applied at different points of the enemy line in succession, the assault being taken up by fresh formations as the battle moved from one flank to the other. The enemy would have to commit reserves to meet each new assault, hopefully taking them from the extreme, and as yet unthreatened

Major General Daniel Harvey Hill's division distinguished itself at Antietam, as indeed it had at Second Manassas and South Mountain earlier. Hill was at the council of war that led to battle at Sharpsburg.

flank, to buttress the portions of his line under attack. The offensive would be culminated by launching a fresh formation against a segment of the enemy line, not yet assaulted, that had been stretched through sending troops to other sectors more immediately threatened. McClellan apparently intended to employ Burnside's IX Corps in this final role. He seems to have thought that Hooker, Mansfield, and Sumner would force Lee to move more and more troops towards his centre and left, and Burnside would attack at the critical moment by crossing the Antietam Creek and driving towards Sharpsburg against minimal opposition. McClellan could then employ his considerable reserve, Porter's V Corps and Franklin's VI Corps, in the final destruction of Lee's army against the Potomac River. This type of general battle plan called for careful timing and constant pressure on the enemy line. The Federal Army of the Potomac would accomplish neither during the Antietam engagement. Lee's Army of Northern Virginia would be able to meet each Federal threat in turn as unplanned lulls occurred in the fighting. Burnside's

◀ *A view of Lee's head-quarters, in the Jacob Grove house, in Sharpsburg. Actually, he used tents for his own and staff* *quarters, and they were pitched in a small grove on the right of the Shepherdstown Road, just outside town.*

peculiar apathy would also contribute significantly to Lee's survival.

During the early stages of the Maryland Campaign, McClellan had given Burnside command of I Corps as well as his own IX Corps, constituting the right wing of the Army of the Potomac. Burnside had directed the South Mountain engagements, acting in the capacity of a wing commander. Burnside was shocked, however, to find that when the Army of the Potomac deployed along the Antietam Creek I Corps (Hooker) formed the extreme right wing of the Army and his IX Corps formed the extreme *left* flank. Burnside's right wing was divided by the remainder of the Army. McClellan did not inform Burnside that he had scrapped the wing arrangement and apparently simply assumed that Burnside would understand that he was once again in command of only IX Corps. It was a fact that Burnside was either not made aware of, or something of which he pretended to take no notice, and the result was considerable command confusion producing unconscionable delay through-

out the battle of 17 September. Burnside claimed that after the death of Major General Jesse Reno at South Mountain the command of IX Corps fell to the commander of the Kanawha Division, Brigadier General Jacob Cox. Cox was uncertain whether he was actually in command of IX Corps, and his uncertainty was hardly eased by an obviously angry Burnside constantly looking over his shoulder. The vital mission of carrying the stone bridge and crossing the Antietam in order to complete the destruction of Lee's army begun by the Federal I, II, and XII Corps was delayed by these personality-induced confusions. The sulky Burnside would not move with any speed, and clearly his demotion from wing commander – in his eyes – eliminated any confidence that he may have had in McClellan's battlefield direction.

▼ *Doubleday's Division of I Corps crosses the upper fords of the Antietam Creek.*

ANTIETAM: HOOKER'S ATTACK

Federal I Corps (Hooker) crossed the Antietam Creek about 1400 on 16 September, advanced south some time after 1600 and made contact with Confederate pickets at dusk. It remained in position facing the extreme Confederate left during the night of 16/17 September. Federal XII Corps (Mansfield) crossed its two divisions after midnight in support of Hooker's formations. It was apparent to the soldiers of both armies that a major battle was about to be fought. 'The fights of the previous days were only preliminaries', wrote Lieutenant Edwin Stone of Battery C/1st Rhode Island Volunteer Light Artillery, 'to the great struggle between constitutional law and the inviolability of the national compact on the one side, and of treason on the other.'

The position of I Corps informed Lee of where the blow was likely to fall in the morning. He had managed to gather all his various forces behind the Antietam Creek by the late afternoon of 16 September, with the exception of A. P. Hill's division, which was in the vicinity of Harper's Ferry. Lee's right and centre were held by Longstreet's divisions. The Confederate left was held by formations commanded by 'Stonewall' Jackson.

I Corps Attacks

There had been skirmishing between Jackson's and Hooker's pickets since darkness fell on 16 September. Federal I Corps began advancing south at dawn (listed as 0543 on 17 September), moving towards the small Dunkard Church with the objective of occupying the higher ground to Hooker's front. The Federals made contact with the Confederate line at approximately 0615. Jackson's left was held by his old division commanded now by Brigadier General John Robert Jones, and his right was formed by Ewell's division, commanded by Brigadier General Alexander Robert Lawton. The Confederate left was supported by the small division commanded by Brigadier General John Hood. Hooker advanced into the North and East Woods with his 1st Division commanded by Brigadier General Abner Doubleday on his right facing Jones,

▶ This woodcut was made from an eye-witness sketch of Hooker's division of I Corps fording the Antietam Creek at 10 a.m. to start the battle. The men wear their greatcoats, apparently to fend off the chilly morning air, although their need seems questionable.

and his 2nd Division commanded by Brigadier General James Ricketts on his left facing Lawton. The Pennsylvania Reserve Division (3rd Division/I Corps) led by Meade formed Hooker's centre, moving slightly behind Doubleday and Ricketts.

'We had not proceeded far', wrote Hooker in his report on Antietam, 'before I discovered that a heavy force of the enemy had taken possession of a cornfield in my immediate front, and from the sun's rays falling on their bayonets projecting above the corn could see that the field was filled with the enemy.' Hooker's troops drove in Jackson's skirmishers and proceeded to push the two Confederate divisions on the Southern left out of the East Woods, beyond the cornfield and into the West Woods. Rickett's division

Private, 1st Infantry Regiment, Reserve Brigade of Philadelphia, which continued wearing grey long after other Federal units changed to blue. During the Antietam campaign, however, they wore dark blue fatigue blouses. Painting by Ron Volstad

made better progress against Lawton's command. Jackson's formations were nearly destroyed during the initial Federal assault.

Lee realized that Jackson's position would collapse unless timely assistance were sent. The failure of McClellan to put pressure along the entirety of the Confederate line permitted Lee to order various formations to Jackson's assistance. Jackson was able, therefore, to employ his reserve formation, the two brigades commanded by Hood. Hood's regiments, particularly his Texas regiments, were rapidly becoming known as the shock troops of Lee's army. At approximately 0700, Hood's two brigades were ordered by Jackson to drive the Federals out of the cornfield and to restore the centre of the Confederate left.

▼ *This post-war print by Lewis Prang shows the Union advance into the cornfield.*

Hood's Counter-Attack

Hood's men were outnumbered, but they were relatively fresh and the Federals did not expect them. 'It was here', wrote Hood in his report, 'that I witnessed the most terrible clash of arms, by far, that has occurred during the War.' Colonel William Tatum Wofford, a pre-war lawyer, newspaper editor and plantation owner commanding Hood's old brigade in the action, wrote of his men: 'They fought desperately; their conduct was never surpassed.' Hood's assault fell on the 'Iron Brigade', 4th Brigade/1st Division/I Corps, commanded by Colonel John Gibbon, who had the 6th Wisconsin on his right and the 2nd Wisconsin on his left. The

◀ *Major General George G. Meade commanded a division in I Corps during the battle; he would eventually receive command of the entire Army of the Potomac and command it at Gettysburg. At Antietam, his men followed Doubleday's, advancing through the North Woods into the cornfield.*

▼ *This church used by members of the Dunker faith, a pacifist group, was on the Hagerstown Road at the edge of the West Woods. The 125th Pennsylvania Infantry entered the woods just on the right of the church, seen here some years after the war.*

Brigadier General John B. Hood's proud Texans of the Texas Brigade suffered the greatest casualties of any unit during the battle, yet held on.

A serving US soldier since 1822, Major General Joseph K. F. Mansfield was mortally wounded while leading his XII Corps forward to support I Corps.

remainder of the brigade formed a second line. Additionally, Gibbon was supported by the 1st Division's 1st Brigade, commanded by Colonel Walter Phelps of the 22nd New York and the 2nd Division's 3rd Brigade commanded by Brigadier General Lucas Hartsuff. Gibbon's men resisted stubbornly. The Federal gunners of Battery B/4th United States Artillery, commanded by Lieutenant James Stewart, shelled the cornfield with spherical case shot and finally gave the advancing rebels canister at close range. Captain Jonathan Callis took his 7th Wisconsin from Gibbon's second line, changed front, and hit Hood's left flank hard. The unexpected attack of the 7th Wisconsin shook Hood's men and 'broke them up badly', wrote Callis, 'scattering them in great confusion.' Hood's officers reformed their men, however, and the desperate battle over Miller's cornfield continued. 'Not one showed any disposition', stated Lieutenant Colonel S. Z. Ruff of the 18th Georgia, 'notwithstanding their terrible loss, to fall back or flinch from the enemy until they received orders to do so.'

Hood's assault had stalled by 0720. The cornfield was only momentarily retaken, but more significantly the force of Hood's counter-attack had stabilized Jackson's position. The conflict on the Confederate left seemed more savage to the participants than any combat experiences they might have had earlier in the War. Hooker wrote in his report: 'The slain lay in rows precisely as they had stood in their ranks a few moments before. It was never my fortune to witness a more bloody, dismal battlefield.'

McClellan's battle plan apparently intended that Hooker's assault be picked up by Federal XII Corps, deploying by 0730 on Hooker's left flank. XII Corps was commanded by Major General Joseph King Fenno Mansfield.

XII Corps Attacks

Mansfield logically assumed on the morning of 17 September, given McClellan's general plan, that his mission was to continue Hooker's successful assault against Lee's left. He had received no information to

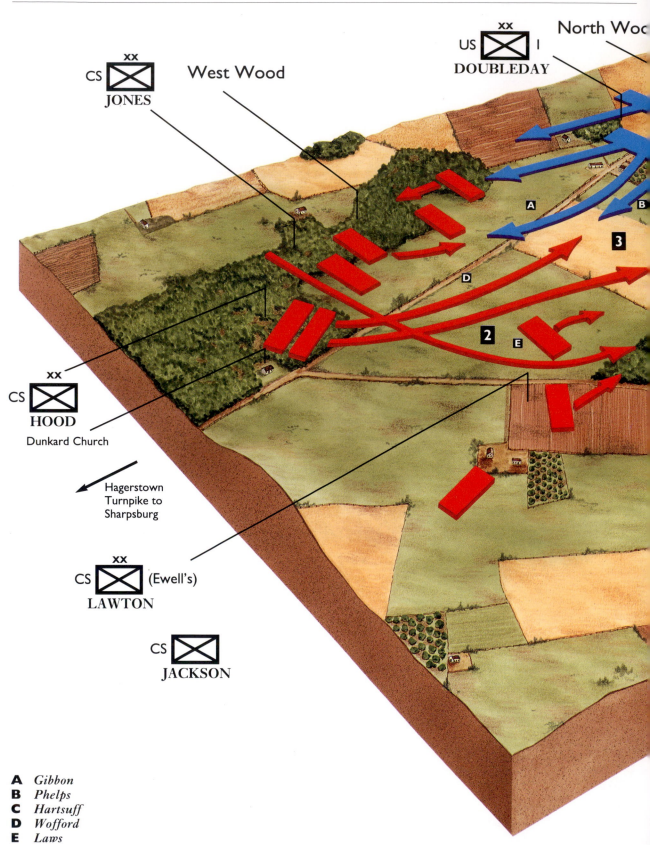

CS **JONES** xx

West Wood

US **DOUBLEDAY** xx I

North Woo

CS **HOOD** xx

Dunkard Church

Hagerstown
Turnpike to
Sharpsburg

CS **LAWTON** xx (Ewell's)

CS **JACKSON** xx

A *Gibbon*
B *Phelps*
C *Hartsuff*
D *Wofford*
E *Laws*

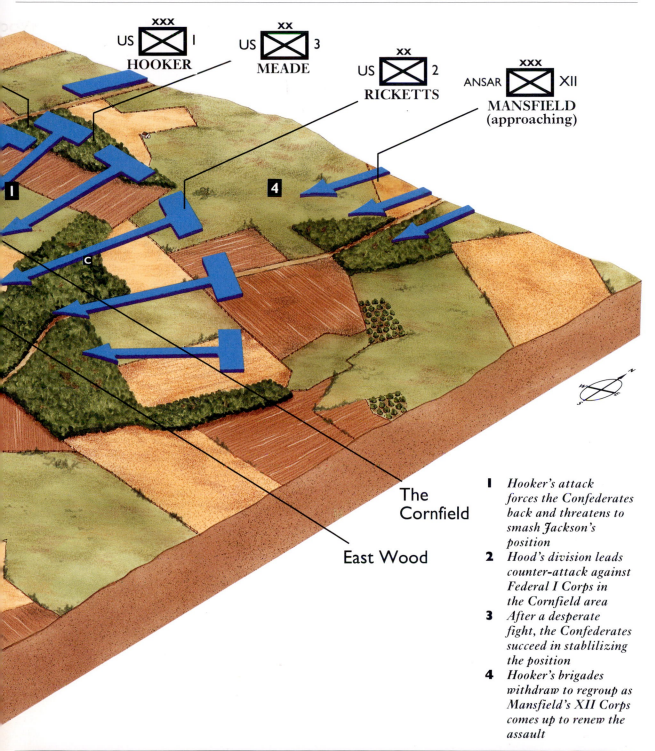

US ⊠ I
HOOKER

US ⊠ 3
MEADE

US ⊠ 2
RICKETTS

ANSAR ⊠ XII
MANSFIELD
(approaching)

The
Cornfield

East Wood

1 *Hooker's attack forces the Confederates back and threatens to smash Jackson's position*

2 *Hood's division leads counter-attack against Federal I Corps in the Cornfield area*

3 *After a desperate fight, the Confederates succeed in stablilizing the position*

4 *Hooker's brigades withdraw to regroup as Mansfield's XII Corps comes up to renew the assault*

ANTIETAM: THE INITIAL ATTACK

Hooker (Federal I Corps) attacks Jackson's position at the left of the Confederate line, and is repulsed by the counter-attack of Hood's division, c.0615–0720 17 September 1862

suggest that things were not going well with the Federal assault. Mansfield was shocked, therefore, when in a fleeting conversation Hooker informed him that counter-attacking Rebels (Hood's division) had broken the centre of his I Corps, and that Mansfield must retrieve the situation immediately with his two divisions. This was not what Mansfield had expected. The excited I Corps commander had convinced Mansfield, however, that he must adopt a defensive posture in the East Woods. It may have seemed to Mansfield that any attempt to continue Hooker's offensive beyond was not a wise course of action. Mansfield attempted to alter his deployment, as his troops were nearly in contact with the enemy. It is small wonder that Mansfield became a bit disoriented.

Mansfield rode to one of his leading regiments, the 10th Maine, as it was about to lead XII Corps formations across the last fence separating open fields from the East Woods. There was an outbreak of rifle fire. Mansfield thought his men were shooting at retreating elements of Federal I Corps, and he ordered the shooting stopped. He was mistaken. They were indeed Confederates, the 20th Georgia Regiment. Mansfield tried to get his horse to jump the fence that stood between him, on the side nearest the enemy, and the 10th Maine, standing quiet now in a ploughed field. The horse refused the fence. Mansfield dismounted and led him around. Lieutenant John McGould, Adjutant of the 10th

▲ *Brigadier General George S. Greene commanded the second division of XII Corps at Antietam, and then later at Chancellorsville and Gettysburg. His troops, led by the 28th* *Pennsylvania, crashed into the Confederates in the cornfield.*
▼ *A panorama of the attack of XII Corps as depicted in the contemporary pages of* **Harper's Weekly.**

Maine, recounted what happened next in a letter to Mansfield's son, Lieutenant Samuel Mather Mansfield. 'He passed to the rear of the regimental line, when a gust of wind blew aside his coat, and I discovered that his whole front was covered with blood. I had watched the General for more than five minutes expecting every moment to see him shot, but this was the first knowledge I had of the accident. I ran to him and asked if he was hurt badly. He said, "Yes, I shall not live, shall not live. I am shot by one of our own men." He was attempting to mount his horse again, but I informed him that the horse was wounded, and suggested his taking the orderly's, but his strength now failed him, and he said, "No, take me off. I am shot. I shall not live", and he directed the orderly to look after his horse.'

Mansfield died later that afternoon. One of his staff officers wrote to the General's wife that after requesting assignment to active duty Mansfield had said, 'Major, I am an old man, and I want to die in defence of the Capitol.' Mansfield had seen that wish come true, but XII Corps now found itself in brief confusion at a key moment in the battle by their general's untimely departure from the field. The command passed to Brigadier General Alpheus Starkey Williams, who commanded XII Corps' 1st Division. Williams received only perfunctory directions from Hooker, who was shortly thereafter wounded in the foot and who then proceeded to retire from the field with an infirmity perhaps more mental than physical. Williams remarked dryly in his report that he had received, 'such directions as the pressing exigencies would permit', and that he had then 'hastened to make a disposition of the Corps to meet them'.

Williams deployed his 1st Division, now led by Brigadier General Samuel Crawford, to his right in order to connect with the left flank of I Corps, driven out of the cornfield by Hood's counterattack. He placed the 2nd Division/XII Corps, commanded by Brigadier General George Sears Greene, to the left. Williams decided that the Federal forces must continue the offensive, whatever the condition of I Corps. He attacked out of the East Woods virtually alone, with only marginal assistance from Hooker's exhausted troops. The two divisions of XII Corps did not move forward in a coordinated fashion. Williams led the 1st Division through the southern portion of the North Woods towards the Confederate positions in the West Woods. He made little headway and suffered heavy casualties. The 2nd Division led by Greene moved out of the East Woods, advancing directly on the Dunkard Church, taking a position close to the structure after bitter fighting at 0800 and holding it for several hours.

II Corps Attacks

The first elements of Federal II Corps began arriving on the battlefield at 0830, the 2nd Division/II

Corps commanded by Major General John Sedgwick. 'Soon after', wrote Williams, 'the firing on both sides wholly ceased.' Williams withdrew his 1st Division towards the North Woods and a lull settled over the battlefield.

Further Federal assistance was about to arrive. McClellan had sent Major General Edwin Sumner, commander of Federal II Corps, orders to cross the Antietam Creek at 0700 on the morning of 17 September. Sumner's orders were to support the advance of I and XII Corps in their assault on the Confederate left. Major General John Sedgwick's 2nd Division/II Corps moved from their camp at 0700 and Brigadier General William French's 3rd Division/II Corps followed at 0730; however, the 1st Division/II Corps led by Brigadier General Israel Richardson did not receive the corps order to advance until 0930. Richardson's men were unaccountably far behind the remainder of the Corps.

Sumner advanced with such military precision, with Sedgwick on the Federal right and French on the left, that the martial display created by Federal

◀ *'Uncle John' Sedgewick, one of the most loved Union commanders, was wounded three times during the battle of Antietam, finally being carried unconscious from the field. He commanded II Corps, which was posted to the right of XII Corps.*

II Corps was much commented on by participants of both sides. Sedgwick moved forward towards the West Woods and the Dunkard Church in three brigade lines: the 1st Brigade commanded by Brigadier General Willis Gorman, the 3rd Brigade commanded by Brigadier General Napoleon Dana, and the 2nd Brigade, known as the 'Philadelphia Brigade' commanded by Brigadier General Oliver Howard. 'Passing through a strip of timber, we entered into a large open field', wrote Gorman in his report of the action, 'which was strewn with the enemy's dead and wounded.' The division commanded by French moved more to the left, against the positions held by the Confederate division commanded by Daniel Harvey Hill. There was an unfortunate gap developing between French and Sedgwick, growing wider as they advanced closer to the Confederate lines.

Federal I and XII Corps were fought out by 0900 when Sumner's two divisions advanced. The situation in Southern ranks was little better – many of Jackson's formations were no longer truly com-

▶ *Major General Edwin V. ('Old Bull') Sumner, the oldest general to hold corps command in either army, had been commissioned in 1819, commanding II Corps. His tactics at Antietam of putting all his men into action, and actively leading the first division instead of staying behind where a man of his rank could be of more service, were highly criticized.*

bat-effective, and the divisions commanded by Jones and Lawton had nearly ceased to exist. Jackson was forced to defend none the less against the arrival of fresh Northern formations. 'Instantly my whole brigade became hotly engaged', wrote Brigadier General Gorman, commanding the first line of Sedgwick's advance, 'giving and receiving the most deadly fire it has ever been my lot to witness.' The Confederate line on Lee's left had been severely strained since dawn and broken in places, but it had held against repeated Federal assaults. The senior Federal generals insisted on attacking piecemeal, permitting effective Southern responses to every Federal forward movement, meeting each new threat as it developed. Lee was able to employ his scant military reserves in the most economical manner. Jackson would need further help, however, if he were to hold against the advance of Federal II Corps.

The McLaws–Walker Counter-Attack

Lee sent the two-brigade division commanded by Brigadier General John Walker from the extreme Confederate right to report to Jackson. The dispatch of Walker's division from the Confederate right meant that only one brigade was being left to oppose the possible advance of Federal IX Corps across Antietam Creek. The conduct of the Federals so far in the engagement regarding the commitment of their reserves and in their apparent unwillingness to launch a coordinated attack led Lee to believe that the gamble of drastically weakening his right was necessary to allow his left to survive. In addition, Lee sent Jackson his only major reserve, the division commanded by Major General Lafayette McLaws, which had been camped at Lee's headquarters near the village of Sharpsburg since its arrival at sunrise. Lafayette McLaws (1821-1897)

▲ *From General McClellan's headquarters, the Pry house (above right), observers could see Sumner's Corps advancing in the middle, with Franklin's VI Corps to his right in support. A column of smoke rises from the Mumma house and barn. Fighting between Mansfield and Jackson takes place in the East Wood, on the extreme right.*

was an 1842 graduate of the United States Military Academy and an officer in the regular army before the War. McLaws had been a first classman at West Point when Jackson had reported as a plebe. As soon as they arrived in his sector, McLaws' and Walker's troops (under McLaws as the senior general officer) were ordered by Jackson to make an immediate counter-attack on Sedgwick's Federal division and drive them out of the West Woods. The assault took place at approximately 1030.

McLaws' division advanced with his brigades commanded in the following order, from left to right: Brigadier General Paul J. Semmes, Brigadier General William Barksdale, Brigadier General Joseph Kershaw and Brigadier General Howell Cobb. Walker's division advanced behind McLaws division as a support, with Brigadier General Robert Ransom's North Carolinian Brigade on the left and Walker's own brigade commanded by Colonel Van H. Manning on the right. Manning detached the 3rd Arkansas and 27th North Carolina regiments to cover the distance between Walker's advance and the left of Longstreet's command. Walker's division drifted more to the right during the advance than perhaps was intended by Jackson, so that it eventually moved beyond McLaws' right. The counter-attacking Rebel divisions 'advanced in splendid style', wrote Walker in his report, 'firing and cheering as they went, and in a few minutes cleared the woods.' McLaws wrote that his advance was 'sweeping the woods with perfect ease and

inflicting great loss on the enemy'. Colonel Manning even advanced beyond the remainder of Walker's division with his 46th North Carolina, 48th North Carolina, and 30th Virginia Regiments. Walker reported that Manning's men were 'driving the enemy like sheep'.

The advance of McLaws and Walker had struck the left flank of Sedgwick's advance, creating considerable confusion. 'The attack of the enemy on the flank was so sudden', wrote Brigadier General Gorman, commanding Sedgwick's first brigade line, 'and in such overwhelming force that I had no time to lose.' Desperate Federal officers tried to rally their men and reform until finally they withdrew and managed to stabilize a new line some 200 yards

◀ *Major General Lafayette McLaws, a Georgian, had received his promotion to divisional commander because of prior services during the Peninsular campaign.*

▼ *General McClellan riding the line of battle. His black horse, named Daniel Webster, was so fast that the Staff had difficulty keeping up and referred to him as 'that Devil Dan'.*

to the rear. There was heavy fighting. 'In this terrible conflict three regiments of the brigade', wrote Gorman, 'the 15th Massachusetts, 34th and 82nd New York Volunteers, lost nearly one-half their entire force engaged.' McLaws and Walker had succeeded in stalling any further advance of Sedgwick's division and had restored solidarity to the sector commanded by Jackson. Fighting would continue throughout the day on the Confederate left, but serious fighting was completed by 1300. The first phase of the battle of Antietam was over.

It did not have to be, however, because Sumner, commander of Federal II Corps, received substantial reinforcements just as the assault of McLaws and Walker was beginning to come to a conclusion. The new formations were the two divisions of Federal VI Corps, led by Major General Franklin, which had remained in the vicinity of Rohrersville following the battle of Crampton's Gap on 14 September. Franklin had been ordered by McClellan on the evening of the 16th to bring VI Corps to the Sharpsburg area after detaching the 1st Division/IV Corps, attached to Franklin's command and led by Major General Darius Couch, to occupy Maryland Heights, presumably to protect the Army of Potomac's communications. Couch's division was wastefully employed and not ordered to join the rest of the Army of the Potomac until the fighting was over. VI Corps arrived on the Antietam battlefield at 1000.

Franklin was ordered to send his leading formation, Major General Smith's 2nd Division/VI Corps, to support Sumner's II Corps. Brigadier General Winfield Hancock's 1st Brigade/2nd Division/VI Corps, deployed at the front of Smith's column, was instrumental in finally halting the Confederate counter-attack. 'This brigade was the means of saving two batteries', wrote Franklin, 'and occupied its position during the remainder of the action, sometimes under very heavy cannonading.' Franklin brought up his other division, the 1st Division/VI Corps commanded by Major General Slocum, at 1100, and deployed his two divisions for an immediate attack on the disorganized Confederate forces to his front. Franklin believed that he had a very good chance of destroying the Confederate left once and for all – and he may have been correct, since Lee had no reserves immediately

Private of the 1st US Sharpshooters, who wore the standard frock coat and trousers but of rifle green rather than of blue wool, and with hard rubber buttons. The weapon is a Sharps rifle. Painting by Michael Youens.

available. Sumner would not, however, allow Franklin to attack. The matter was referred to McClellan, who selected a cautious approach and supported Sumner's position. VI Corps did not advance, and McClellan may have lost his best opportunity to win a decisive victory at Antietam. Franklin remarked in his report with commendable restraint, 'The commanding general came to the position and decided that it would not be prudent to make the attack.'

ANTIETAM: BLOODY LANE

Major General William French's 3rd Division/II Corps had advanced on the left of Sedgwick's command when Sumner initially led II Corps forward. Sedgwick's men advanced on the West Woods, and French's troops moved more to the south against a sunken farm lane defended by Major General Daniel Harvey Hill's Confederate division. The position defended by Hill has come to be known as 'bloody lane', and it provided the Confederates with a naturally strong defensive position.

Daniel Harvey Hill's Confederate Division had been heavily engaged at South Mountain, and casualties there along with the straggling that had plagued the Army of Northern Virginia throughout the Maryland Campaign had severely depleted Hill's brigades. Garland's Brigade had been nearly eliminated at South Mountain, and it along with Ripley's Brigade had been sent earlier in the day to assist Jackson around the time of Hood's morning counterattack. Hill had the remains of Colquitt's Brigade in the sunken road with its left flank on the Hagerstown Road, followed from left to right by Rodes' Alabamian Brigade and George B. Anderson's North Carolinian Brigade. The Confederate

▼ *The south-eastern section of the sunken road, as seen in 1885.*

line in the sunken road was continued by two brigades of Richard Anderson's Division, those commanded by Brigadier General Ambrose Wright and Colonel Alfred Cuming (Wilcox's Brigade). The remainder of Anderson's Division, commanded now by Brigadier General Robert Pryor, formed behind the sunken road as Hill's reserve, the brigades of: Brigadier General Winfield Feather-ston, Pryor's Brigade commanded by its senior Colonel, and fragments of two Virginia brigades.

Hill was further supported beyond the sunken road, to the right by the independent brigade commanded by Brigadier General Nathan 'Shanks' Evans. The South Carolinians with Evans represented some of the most blue blooded of the Palmetto State's aristocracy. The next Confederate formation to the right was the division commanded by Brigadier General David R. Jones of Longstreet's command, which thinly stretched the Confederate line towards the Burnside Bridge area.

▶ *Because the Union attacks were totally un-coordinated, Lee was able to use his interior lines to rush troops from one threatened part of the field to another. Here he and one of his divisional commanders, Daniel H. Hill, ride along their lines during a respite in fighting on this sector of the front.*

The Initial Attacks

French advanced his Division in three lines with Brigadier General Max Weber's 3rd Brigade in front, followed by the 2nd Brigade commanded by Colonel Dwight Morris, and the 1st Brigade in the rear led by Brigadier General Nathan Kimball. French was informed of Sedgwick's difficulties and lengthened his line by advancing Kimball, ordering him to form on the left of Weber. Kimball's Brigade advanced with the 14th Indiana on his right and connected with Weber's regiments, followed from right to left by the 8th Ohio, 7th West Virginia, and 132nd Pennsylvania regiments. 'Directly on my front', reported Kimball, 'in a narrow road running parallel with my line, and, being washed by water, forming a natural rifle pit between my line and a large cornfield, I found the enemy in great force.'

Kimball's men were opposite the part of the sunken road held by Colquitt, Rodes, and G. B. Anderson. Hill's men had the advantage of a strong defensive position. In addition, the advancing Federals of French's division could not have seen the 'sunken road' until they were practically on top of it. The fighting was severe as French's men tried to carry the Confederate position and, failing in the attempt, then struggled to retain their own position before it.

Kimball's men stood their ground. 'Every man of my command behaved in the most exemplary manner', wrote Kimball, 'as men who had determined to save their country or die.'

The 2nd Brigade/3rd Division was composed of freshly raised troops; Antietam was their first battle. The 14th Connecticut had never fired their weapons before, and although the regiment would participate in twenty-three separate major engagements and serve in all the actions of the Army of the Potomac to the end of the War, many would recall 17 September as a harsh introduction to the conflict. 'Our colors are riddled with shot and shell', wrote Lieutenant Colonel Sanford Perkins, 'and the staff broken.' He added with pride in his report to his superiors, 'As you are aware, our men, hastily raised and without drill, behaved like veterans, and fully maintained the honor of the Union and our native State.' French was unable to drive Hill out of the sunken road, but Hill was equally unable to drive French away from it.

French received reinforcements ultimately from Brigadier Israel Richardson's 1st Division/II Corps, the first formation of which, forming to French's left, was the 'Irish Brigade' (2nd Brigade/1st Division/II Corps). The Irish regiments were commanded by Thomas Francis Meagher (1823–67), a colourful character born in Ireland, who was ordered transported to Tasmania in 1849 by English authorities on charges of seditious activities. Meagher had managed to find his way to America before the War and in the immediate pre-war era he became a recognized leader among the Irish-American population in New York City. Meagher had raised his command from the ethnically Irish population of New York City and other north-eastern urban communities. He now deployed his 69th New York to the right, connecting with French's troops, followed from right to left by the 29th Massachusetts, 63rd New York and the 88th New York. The 1st Brigade/1st Division/II Corps, commanded by Brigadier General John Caldwell, formed to Meagher's left. Richardson retained his 3rd Brigade under Colonel John Brooke in a second

◀ *French's Division sweeps forward against the Roulette House and*

Barns, while Richardson's Division attacks the sunken road on the left.

line as a reserve. Richardson's formations were opposite Wright's and Wilcox's brigades, the latter commanded by Colonel Cuming, both of Anderson's Confederate Division. The Irish regiments of Meagher's Brigade advanced under their prominent green regimental battle-flags to 'within paces of the enemy', where they were halted to trade rifle volleys with the Confederates. 'On coming into this close and fatal contact with the enemy', wrote Meagher, 'the officers and the men of the brigade waved their swords and hats and gave the heartiest cheers for their general, George B. McClellan, and the Army of the Potomac.' Meagher advanced his right two regiments slightly in an attempt to carry the Confederate line but was unable to make any headway against the torrent of musketry delivered at him by Hill's troops. The Irish Brigade was decimated and sent to the rear. Caldwell's brigade was

redeployed by Richardson to cover Meagher's withdrawal.

The struggle over the sunken road and the orchard behind it lasted three and a half hours, from approximately 0930 to some time after 1300. There were a number of charges and counter-charges launched by both sides, as the Federal divisions commanded by French and Richardson contended for the possession of the 'bloody lane' with Hill's and Anderson's Confederate brigades. 'The battle raged incessantly', wrote Brigadier General Kimball, 'without either party giving way.'

The Exposed Flank

Brigadier General Rodes attempted to take advantage of a gap between Kimball and Caldwell's commands, taking several Southern regiments against

◀ *The sunken road, looking east from the lane leading to the Roulette house, as seen in 1885.*

Kimball's left. Kimball countered this movement by changing the front of his left regiments, the 7th West Virginia and the 132nd Pennsylvania. He received assistance from Colonel John R. Brooke, commanding the 3rd Brigade/1st Division/II Corps, who changed the front of the 2nd Delaware and 52nd New York Regiments and ordered a charge of his own regiment, the 53rd Pennsylvania. Rodes was forced to retire to his original position in the sunken road. Brigadier General Caldwell, commanding the 1st Brigade of Richardson's division, meanwhile succeeded in driving Wright's Brigade and Colonel Cuming's command out of the right portion, from the Confederate perspective, of the sunken road.

The situation turned dismal for Rodes' command in an instant. Anderson's men were retreating out of the sunken road, Caldwell's men were advancing, and Rodes found his right, which remained in the sunken road, exposed to a flank attack. Rodes was informed of this difficulty by the excited commander of the 6th Alabama, Lieutenant Colonel James M. Lightfoot. Lightfoot's men were now the extreme right flank of that portion of the sunken road retained by the Confederates, and Lightfoot told Rodes that his men were 'exposed to a terrible enfilade fire'. The consolidated 61st and 64th New York regiments commanded by Colonel Francis Barlow, the right regiment of Caldwell's Brigade, were the culprits. Rodes ordered Lightfoot to refuse his right; that is, as Rodes said in his report, 'throwing his right wing back and out of the road referred to'. Lightfoot apparently misunderstood and, instead of executing the manoeuvre Rodes envisaged, ordered his regiment to about face and leave the sunken road entirely. The commander

▶ *The sunken road, as seen from the second bend in the lane looking towards the Hagerstown Pike.*

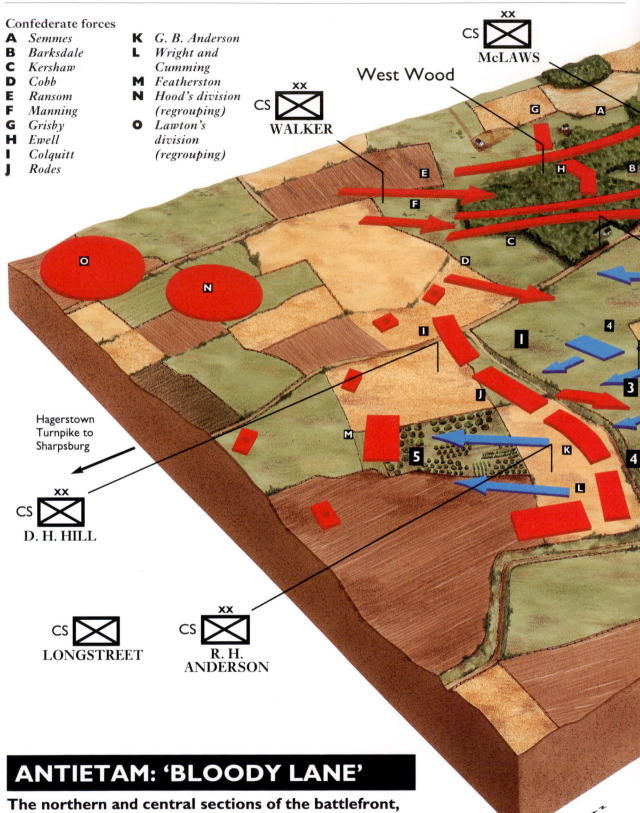

Confederate forces

A *Semmes*
B *Barksdale*
C *Kershaw*
D *Cobb*
E *Ransom*
F *Manning*
G *Grisby*
H *Ewell*
I *Colquitt*
J *Rodes*
K *G. B. Anderson*
L *Wright and Cumming*
M *Featherston*
N *Hood's division (regrouping)*
O *Lawton's division (regrouping)*

CS — McLAWS

CS — WALKER

West Wood

Hagerstown Turnpike to Sharpsburg

CS — D. H. HILL

CS — LONGSTREET

CS — R. H. ANDERSON

ANTIETAM: 'BLOODY LANE'

The northern and central sections of the battlefront, c.0930 to 1300 17 September, showing the attack of Federal II Corps on the sunken road.

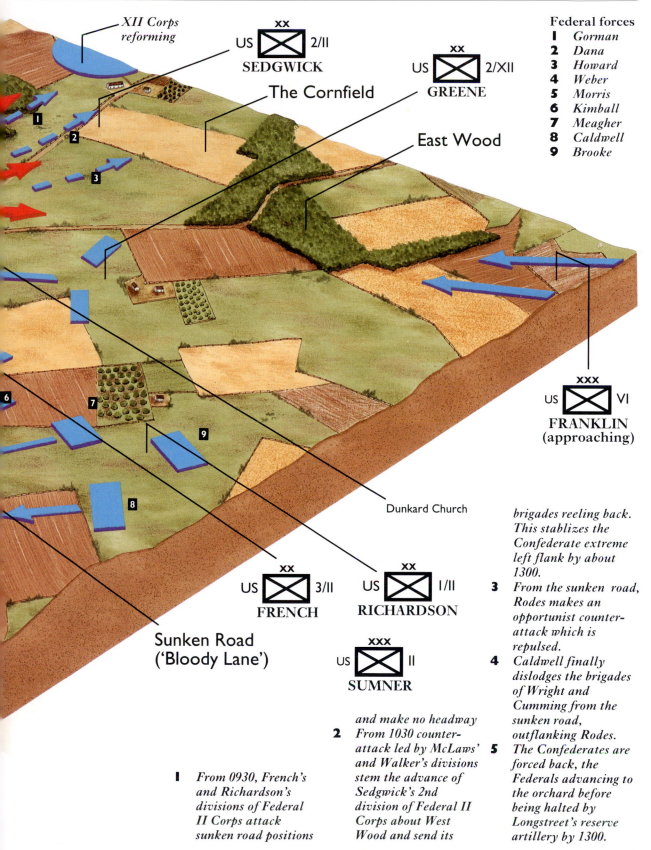

XII Corps
reforming

US **2/II**
SEDGWICK

The Cornfield

US **2/XII**
GREENE

East Wood

Federal forces
1 *Gorman*
2 *Dana*
3 *Howard*
4 *Weber*
5 *Morris*
6 *Kimball*
7 *Meagher*
8 *Caldwell*
9 *Brooke*

US **VI**
FRANKLIN
(approaching)

Dunkard Church

US **3/II**
FRENCH

US **I/II**
RICHARDSON

US **II**
SUMNER

Sunken Road
('Bloody Lane')

*brigades reeling back.
This stablizes the
Confederate extreme
left flank by about
1300.*

3 *From the sunken road,
Rodes makes an
opportunist counter-
attack which is
repulsed.*

4 *Caldwell finally
dislodges the brigades
of Wright and
Cumming from the
sunken road,
outflanking Rodes.*

5 *The Confederates are
forced back, the
Federals advancing to
the orchard before
being halted by
Longstreet's reserve
artillery by 1300.*

and make no headway

2 *From 1030 counter-
attack led by McLaws'
and Walker's divisions
stem the advance of
Sedgwick's 2nd
division of Federal II
Corps about West
Wood and send its*

1 *From 0930, French's
and Richardson's
divisions of Federal
II Corps attack
sunken road positions*

67

▲ *Fighting was fierce around the ruins of the Mumma house and barns, which had been previously destroyed by D. H. Hill's troops. None the less, wounded men took shelter in what remained of the buildings.*

▶ *Smith's Division of VI Corps charged forward to aid French's badly battered troops, sending Irwin's Brigade against Confederates near the Dunker Church.*

of the regiment to Lightfoot's immediate left, Major Lafayette Hobson of the 5th Alabama, asked Lightfoot in amazement if the order was intended for the entire brigade. Lightfoot replied in the affirmative, and Hobson took the 5th Alabama out of the sunken road also. Rodes' men promptly abandoned their position, to the astonishment of their brigade commander.

The commander of the Federal forces immediately opposite Rodes, Brigadier General Kimball, ordered an advance and took possession of the sunken road as Rodes' Confederates deserted it. Kimball and Barlow claimed 300 Southern prisoners and a number of Confederate colours. The remaining formations of Anderson's Confederate Division, now commanded by Brigadier General Pryor, should have been available to halt further

Federal progress, but Pryor's men apparently merged with other retreating Confederates. It is a little uncertain what happened to these units, as no reports are extant in the Official Records from any of the principals of Anderson's division, but what is certain is that they made no real attempt to impede Kimball and Caldwell's advance. There was little left to stop the Federals, except Longstreet's reserve artillery and whatever Southern infantry could be rallied by D. H. Hill and Robert Rodes.

There was further severe fighting as the Federals tried to advance through the orchard and on to the high ground to their front. Kimball was attacked on his right by a number of Southern formations, which he dealt with by refusing the right of the 14th Indiana and the 8th Ohio regiments. Caldwell was attacked on his left by scattered Confederate soldiers led forward personally by Hill. 'Affairs looked very critical,' wrote Hill in his report. The 5th New Hampshire commanded by Colonel Edward Cross was the regiment on Caldwell's left. Cross perceived the danger represented by Hill's assault: 'I instantly ordered a change of front to the rear', he wrote in his report, 'which was executed in time to confront the advancing line of the enemy in their center with a volley at

◀ *Major General Israel B. Richardson was mortally wounded by artillery during the attack through the cornfield.*

▶ *Nelson A. Miles served as lieutenant colonel of the 61st New York Infantry Regiment during the battle of Antietam, taking command of the regiment after its colonel, Francis C. Barlow, was disabled at that battle. The regiment was one of two that swept the Sunken Road with fire and finally took the position.*

very short range, which staggered and hurled them back.' Cross and his men were rewarded by the capture of the state colour of the 4th North Carolina. The vigilant Colonel Barlow deflected a Confederate assault on Caldwell's right, but the Federal troops were fought out and no further advance seemed possible in the face of a severe artillery fire put up by Longstreet's reserve artillery directly in front of Kimball and Caldwell. Major General Richardson was mortally wounded at this stage by a Confederate shell.

The Federals had succeeded in driving the Confederates out of the sunken road, and they had advanced beyond it, but that is all their remaining strength was capable of. The situation was also bad for various Southern formations; indeed, to call

▶ *Confederate dead of D. H. Hill's division lie where they fell, in the sunken road – a near contemprary engraving based on a photograph.*

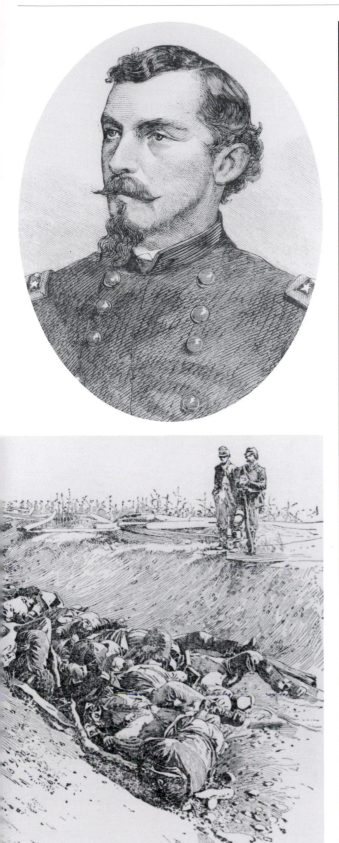

Surgeon of the Confederate Army wearing regulation dress. His sword is a cavalry officer's sabre. Painting by Ron Volstad.

what remained of Hill's and Anderson's formations 'brigades' and 'regiments' was now ludicrous. The Confederates had, however, held the centre of their line. It was shortly after 1300, and the second phase of the Battle of Antietam was over. From this point, attention would settle on the Federal left, where Burnside's IX Corps faced a stone bridge over the Antietam Creek and threatened to assault Lee's right.

ANTIETAM: BURNSIDE BRIDGE

The evidence suggests that McClellan intended Burnside to advance across the Antietam Creek after I, XII, and II Federal Corps had severely weakened the Confederate line and had forced Lee to commit all his available reserves. Burnside would then be in a position to drive the right of Lee's army beyond the village of Sharpsburg, prevent his retreat across the Potomac, and complete his destruction by driving the Confederate forces against McClellan's other formations, supported by the as yet uncommitted V Corps. In order to com-

plete this mission, Burnside should have had his corps across Antietam Creek, deployed, and ready to advance no later than noon.

McClellan claimed in his post-war writing that he ordered Burnside at 0800 on 17 September to 'carry the bridge, then to gain possession of the heights beyond, and to advance along the crest upon Sharpsburg'. If McClellan dispatched the order as he stated, and if Burnside received it by 0930, IX Corps should have been in position by noon. McClellan asserted further in his memoirs that

when it became apparent there was no activity on Burnside's front he sent an aide to discover why, who returned reporting that 'little progress had been made'. McClellan states that he sent a second aide, who eventually delivered the same report. An exasperated McClellan then ordered his Inspector General, Lieutenant Colonel William Sackett, to join Burnside and remain until the commander-in-chief's orders had been carried out and Burnside's men were across the Antietam.

◀ Below left: This drawing made from an 1885 photograph shows the heights to the left where Cobb's troops commanded the Burnside bridge. There were no buildings at that time, and the ground on the hillside was then covered with trees, adding cover for the defence.

▼ This is the view Confederate defenders had of the bridge, showing how exposed it was to enemy fire.

Burnside states in his report that he received an order from McClellan to carry the stone bridge to his front early in the morning; however, Burnside adds that McClellan's order also contained the qualifying statement, 'await further orders before making the attack'. Burnside admits receiving an order to attack at 1000, but it would be 1300 before his leading regiments were actually over the bridge, and it would be 1500 before IX Corps was prepared to advance on Sharpsburg. Burnside should have been attacking towards Sharpsburg around 1300, in order to take full advantage of the severe fighting on Lee's left and centre, concluding at approximately this time. The Antietam Creek may not appear to the casual visitor as a military obstacle today, but it represented precisely that in 1862 to troops attempting to manage their equipment, cross a stream of uncertain depth, and ascend the steep, slippery opposite bank in the face of enemy rifle fire. In addition, jus-

tice to Burnside demands that it be pointed out the forcing of a defended river line is perhaps one of the most difficult operations known to military science.

Burnside refused to admit that he was no longer a wing commander. He preferred to believe that the commander of the Kanawha Division, Brigadier General Jacob Cox, was actually in command of IX Corps. Burnside insisted on sharing tactical command on the field with Cox, as the other formation of his 'wing', I Corps, was on the extreme Federal *right* flank. Burnside wrote in his report, 'General Cox was retained in temporary command of the IX Army Corps, which was the only portion of my command then with me, and my orders were to a great extent given directly to him.' The command situation was, to say the least, confusing.

The Crossing

IX Corps took up position facing Antietam Creek after 0700, with the 2nd Division/IX Corps, commanded by Brigadier General Samuel Sturgis, supported by Colonel George Crook's 2nd Brigade/the Kanawha Division/IX Corps, directly opposite the stone bridge. Brigadier General Isaac Rodman's 3rd Division/IX Corps, minus the 2nd Brigade's 11th Connecticut Regiment deployed as skirmishers in front of Sturgis, was three-quarters of a mile to Burnside's left, looking for a practical ford and constituting the extreme left of the Army of the Potomac. Rodman was supported by the other formation of the Kanawha Division, Colonel Eliakam Scammon's 1st Brigade. The 1st Division/IX Corps, commanded by Brigadier General Orlando Willcox, was kept to the rear and slightly to the right as a reserve. Cox placed the artillery batteries of IX Corps to cover approaches to the stone bridge.

◀ *Top: Errors abound in this impression of the crossing of the Burnside Bridge. Union troops would not have worn greatcoats in the seasonable September weather, while the Confederates were not actually on the bridge itself, but defended it from the heights above.*

◀ *Below: This picture rather more accurately shows the 51st Pennsylvania and 51st New York Regiments actually carrying the bridge after the 2nd Maryland and 6th New Hampshire had been destroyed by enemy fire in the attempt.*

First Lieutenant, 69th New York State Militia Regiment, with the colour that was carried until late in 1862. This regiment was part of the 'Irish Brigade' that attacked the sunken road position at Antietam. Painting by Ron Volstad.

Burnside wrote in his report that he received the order to take the stone bridge at 1000 and that he ordered the 11th Connecticut forward as skirmishers to drive the Confederates away from the foot of the bridge. In addition, he had ordered Colonel Crook to make the actual assault. Burnside also ordered Brigadier General Rodman to find a ford further downstream, cross his division and attack the Confederate extreme right on the far bank. Cox places these events at 0900. It was discovered that Crook's position made an assault impractical, and the mission was assigned to Brigadier General Sturgis's 2nd Division. Sturgis advanced the 2nd Maryland and 6th New Hampshire regiments of his 1st Brigade towards the bridge. It was a daunting task. The road beyond the bridge was 'covered by rifle pits and breastworks', wrote Cox, 'made of rails and stone, all of which defenses, as well as the woods which covered the slope, were filled with the enemy's infantry and sharpshooters.'

The Confederates holding these positions at this time amounted to only a single brigade commanded by Brigadier General Robert Toombs, an

▲ This war-time popular print has incorporated something from the battlefield which actually existed – the Burnside

Bridge – but fails to show the heights above it and, moreover, shows Confederate artillery as its primary defender.

element of D. R. Jones's division. Toombs was one of the 'political generals' that caused so many difficulties for the regular officers serving in both armies. He served in the United States House of Representatives and in the US Senate. Toombs became a leading secessionist in Georgia, was nearly elected president of the Confederacy, and was initially Secretary of State in the Confederate government. He resigned to accept a brigadier generalship, although he had absolutely no military experience. Toombs wanted to lead troops, and he would do so magnificently at Antietam. He placed the 20th Georgia near the bridge, extending his line to the right with the 2nd Georgia and the 50th Georgia regiments (the latter of Drayton's brigade), in an effort to cover the approach from the lower ford. Toombs would receive reinforcements later in the

▲ In this view, the two New York and Pennsylvania regiments have finally crossed the Burnside Bridge and are forming to move up to push the Georgia defenders off the heights above them.

action, the 15th Georgia and the 17th Georgia of his own brigade, and the 11th Georgia of George Anderson's Brigade.

The 2nd Maryland and the 6th New Hampshire advanced, wrote Burnside, 'in the most gallant style'. Colonel Henry Walter Kingsbury's 11th Connecticut, deployed in skirmishing order, tried to support the attacking regiments with rifle fire. Colonel Kingsbury fell mortally wounded, wrote Cox, 'cheering his men on to duty'. The Federal regiments were unable to carry the bridge, however, despite repeated attempts. The volume of musketry delivered by Toombs's Georgians forced their retreat. 'They made a handsome effort', wrote Sturgis, 'but the fire was so heavy on them before they could reach the bridge that they were forced to give way and fall back.'

Sturgis passed the assignment of taking the stone bridge to the commander of his 2nd Brigade, Brigadier Edward Ferrero. He selected the 51st Pennsylvania to make the initial rush over the bridge, followed immediately by the 51st New York, and then the remainder of the brigade. Colonel John

Frederick Hartranft (1830–89), a Pennsylvanian lawyer, led his 51st Pennsylvania over the bridge, supported closely by the 51st New York led by Colonel Robert Brown Potter (1829–87), also a lawyer before the War. The two regiments were actually intermingled so much that their regimental standards reached the opposite slope more or less together. Their divisional commander, Brigadier General Sturgis, wrote that the bridge was taken 'with an impetuosity which the enemy could not resist, and the Stars and Stripes were planted on the opposite bank at 1 o'clock p.m., amid the most enthusiastic cheering from every part of the field where they could be seen'.

Burnside began to consolidate his position on the far bank. Ferrero rushed the remaining regiments of his brigade, the 35th Massachusetts and

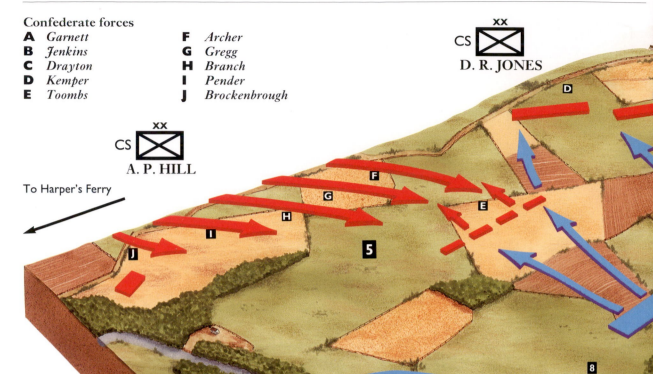

Confederate forces

A *Garnett*
B *Jenkins*
C *Drayton*
D *Kemper*
E *Toombs*
F *Archer*
G *Gregg*
H *Branch*
I *Pender*
J *Brockenbrough*

CS **xx** D. R. JONES

CS **xx** A. P. HILL

To Harper's Ferry

Snavely's Ford

Antietam Creek

I *Nagle's 1st Brigade of Sturgis's 2nd Division attacks the stone bridge but is repulsed*

2 *Sturgis's 2nd Brigade (Ferrero) takes bridge by 1300 and is followed across by Nagle, Crooke and Wilcox's 1st Division*

3 *Meanwhile Rodman's 3rd Division fords at Snavely's Ford*

4 *There is a lull untill 1500 when Wilcox and*

Rodman with Sturgis in rear are ready to attack. The attack reaches the outskirts of Sharpsburg

5 *Hill's division arrives by 1600 and launches vigorous attack on Rodman's flank*

6 *Scammon's Brigade of Kanawha Division comes up to stabilize the situation by 1630 (not shown)*

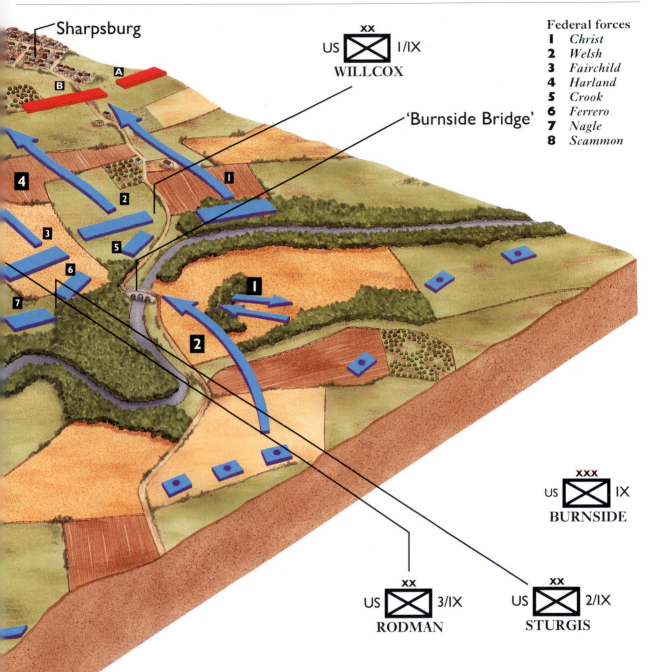

Sharpsburg

US [XX I/IX] **WILLCOX**

'Burnside Bridge'

Federal forces
1 *Christ*
2 *Welsh*
3 *Fairchild*
4 *Harland*
5 *Crook*
6 *Ferrero*
7 *Nagle*
8 *Scammon*

US [XXX IX] **BURNSIDE**

US [XX 3/IX] **RODMAN**

US [XX 2/IX] **STURGIS**

ANTIETAM: 'BURNSIDE BRIDGE'

The southern sector of the battlefield, 0900 to 1630 17 September 1862, showing Burnside's crossing of the Antietam Creek and the intervention of A. P. Hill's division

the 21st Massachusetts, over the bridge in the wake of his other advancing formations. Sturgis brought the 1st Brigade over, followed by Colonel Crook's brigade of the Kanawha Division. Brigadier General Rodman's 3rd Division had managed to cross the ford below the bridge and was also across the stream. Willcox eventually crossed the bridge with his 1st Division.

The Attack on Sharpsburg

Burnside needed time to sort out his formations on the far bank, and additional time was employed in distributing fresh ammunition. IX Corps was not ready to advance on Sharpsburg until 1500. Willcox's 1st Division formed the right, supported by Colonel Crook's brigade of the Kanawha Division. Rodman's 3rd Division formed the left, supported by the other brigade of the Kanawha Division, that commanded by Colonel Scammon. The exhausted troops of Sturgis's 2nd Division were left in the vicinity of the stone bridge. Burnside's men were, nevertheless, over Antietam Creek and advancing. The Confederate division commanded by Brigadier General David Jones was too thinly spread to stop Wilcox's advance, and there was virtually nothing in front of Rodman.

▲ Burnside's men, after taking the heights overlooking the bridge that bears his name, drew up in line of battle ready to attack towards Sharpsburg, as sketched by this eyewitness.

Hill to the Rescue

Lee had no more reserves until the providential arrival of A. P. Hill's 'Light' Division. Hill's men had been processing the captured Federal material at Harper's Ferry, and they were the only major element of the Army of Northern Virginia not yet present on the Antietam battlefield. They arrived in the best American tradition, like the cavalry, to save the situation quite literally at the last possible moment.

At Harper's Ferry, Hill had received orders from Lee at 0630 on 17 September to bring his men immediately to Sharpsburg. Leaving Colonel Edward Thomas's Georgian Brigade at Harper's Ferry to complete business there, Hill had the remainder of his division on the road by 0730 for a march of seventeen miles. The leading elements of the division approached Sharpsburg by 1430, but the division was not ready to advance into combat until 1600, Hill's officers needing time to redeploy their men from marching columns into battle lines.

Brigadier General Isaac P. Rodman got his men over an upper ford above the Burnside Bridge just in time to be attacked by A. P. Hill's arriving Confederates. He was mortally wounded bringing up the 4th Rhode Island Infantry as the 16th Connecticut fell apart under the enemy's attack.

Hill rode ahead of his men to be informed by Lee and David Jones about the precarious position of the Confederate right as a result of Burnside's activities. It was not until after Burnside had advanced and driven back portions of Jones's right that Hill's men were ready to commit themselves to battle. Hill's division advanced with his left brigade connecting with Jones's right flank, his formations deployed from left to right in the following order: Brigadier General James Archer's brigade, Brigadier General Maxey Gregg's brigade, Brigadier General Lawrence Branch's brigade, Brigadier General Dorsey Pender's brigade and Colonel Brockenbrough's brigade. Brockenbrough and Pender now held the extreme Confederate right. The other three brigades, those of Archer, Gregg, and Branch, advanced, wrote Hill, 'with a yell of defiance'. Hill added with something of an understatement that his men were not 'a moment too soon'.

Willcox had advanced his 1st Division/IX Corps from the stone bridge area at 1500 with Colonel Benjamin Christ's 1st Brigade on the right and Colonel Thomas Welsh's 2nd Brigade on the left, Christ deploying the 79th New York as skirmishers, and Welsh employing the 100th Pennsylvania in the same role. These two regiments led the advance of Willcox's Division, which reached the outskirts of Sharpsburg, overrunning several rebel field pieces and generally giving D. R. Jones's Confederate Division some bad moments. Rodman moved his 3rd Division/IX Corps forward with Colonel Harrison Fairchild's 1st Brigade on the right and Colonel Edward Harland's 2nd Brigade the left. Fairchild's men connected with the left of Willcox's division and Harland's command constituted the left of IX Corps. Colonel Crook's 2nd Brigade/the Kanawha Division supported Willcox, and Colonel Scammon's 1st Brigade/the Kanawha Division supported Rodman.

Hill's main assault struck Rodman's division. Harland's brigade was particularly hard hit. The regiments of Harland's command were not in proper order when Hill attacked, the 8th Connecticut on the right being in advance of the other two formations (from right to left, the 16th Connecticut and the 4th Rhode Island). Colonel Frank Beach tried to change the front of the 16th

◀ Two views, the upper version by an eye-witness, of the charge of the 9th New York, Hawkin's Zouaves, of Burnside's division, on a Confederate battery towards the end of the battle. By then it was too late – A. P. Hill was on hand.

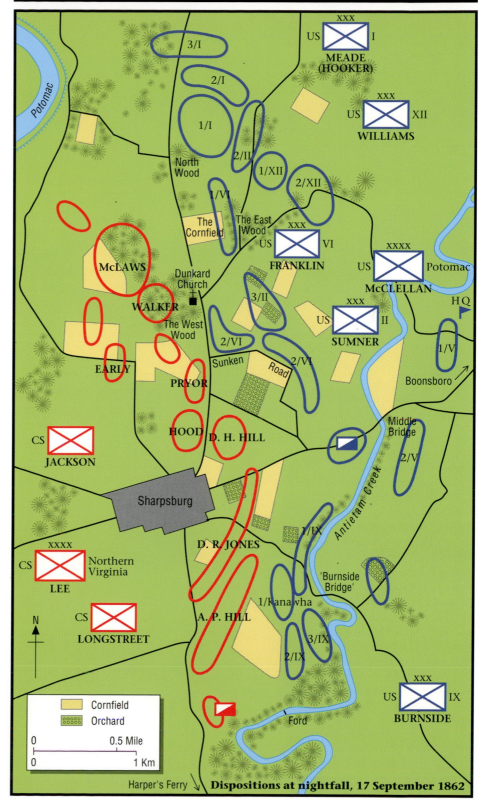

Antietam: Final Dispositions

MEADE
(HOOKER)

WILLIAMS

3/I

2/I

1/I

North
Wood

2/II

1/XII

2/XII

1/VI

The
Cornfield

The East
Wood

FRANKLIN

McLAWS

Dunkard
Church

WALKER

3/II

SUMNER

The West
Wood

2/VI

2/VI

EARLY

Sunken   Road

PRYOR

McCLELLAN

Potomac

HQ

1/V

Boonsboro

HOOD

D. H. HILL

Middle
Bridge

2/V

Antietam Creek

Sharpsburg

1/IX

D. R. JONES

CS
JACKSON

CS
Northern
Virginia

LEE

CS
LONGSTREET

N

A. P. HILL

1/Kanawha

'Burnside
Bridge'

3/IX

2/IX

BURNSIDE

Ford

Cornfield

Orchard

0   0.5 Mile

0   1 Km

Harper's Ferry

Dispositions at nightfall, 17 September 1862

Connecticut by moving to the left to meet Hill's advance, which widened the gap between Beach's men and the 8th Connecticut. The 16th Connecticut was a new formation, and Antietam was its first battle. In fairly short order, confusion reigned. Matters were further confused by the fact that many of Hill's men were wearing parts of Federal uniforms captured at Harper's Ferry. Harland attempted to retrieve the situation by directing the rifle fire of the 8th Connecticut at Hill's advance. The 4th Rhode Island was disordered by the 16th Connecticut's retreat and found itself flanked on the left by more of Hill's troops. The 4th Rhode Island broke, and Harland's Brigade went to the rear.

The situation was saved by the 1st Brigade of the Kanawha Division. Colonel Scammon refused his left flank, placing the 12th Ohio and the 23rd Ohio perpendicular to his other regiment, the 30th Ohio. Scammon's Brigade replaced Harland's in the 3rd Division's line. Burnside ordered Sturgis's 2nd Division from the stone bridge area to buttress the Federal line. It was nearly sunset. IX Corps managed to stop Hill's counter-attack and hold its line. The fighting ended with Willcox's 1st Division/IX Corps on the Federal right, the Kanawha Division under Colonel Scammon in the centre, and Sturgis's 2nd Division/IX Corps holding the left. Fairchild's 1st Brigade/3rd Division/IX Corps was supporting Sturgis, while Harland was trying to reorganize his 2nd Brigade/3rd Division/IX Corps near the stone bridge. Even though some fighting continued after darkness, the third and final phase of the battle of Antietam had concluded.

Major General Fitz John Porter (above), commanding V Corps, could have made the difference in the battle and taken Antietam Bridge (right, a post-war photograph showing a Union wagon train crossing); as it was, the bridge played a minor role in the battle. Instead, Porter advised McClellan against committing his men, since they were the army's only reserve. For this and inactivity earlier he was relieved in November and dismissed from the army. He spent the rest of his life trying to clear his name, finally being placed on the Army Register as colonel of infantry in 1886.

AFTERMATH

The armies remained in position facing each other through the following day, but by the late afternoon of 18 September Lee was making preparations to withdraw the Army of Northern Virginia back to Virginia. Lee's army completed the crossing of the Potomac River near Shepherdstown, West Virginia, on 19 September. A. P. Hill's division was employed again at Boteler's Ford near Shepherdstown on the morning of 20 September to secure the retreat of Lee's reserve artillery. There was no really effective pursuit of Lee by the Army of the Potomac. The Maryland Campaign was over.

The battle of Antietam, Maryland, is correctly referred to as the single bloodiest day of the American Civil War. There were more casualties on 17 September 1862 than any recorded on any other field on any other day during the conflict. The Civil War statistician Thomas L. Livermore states that the Army of the Potomac suffered 2,108 dead, 9,549 wounded, 753 missing, for a total of 12,410 casualties. Livermore puts Confederate loses at 2,700 dead, 9,024 wounded, 2,000 missing, for a total of 13,724 casualties. This represents 26,134 casualties in a single day, more casualties than that suffered by the United States during the entire war with Mexico between 1846 and 1847. The United States Army had 1,721 combat deaths in Mexico, suffered 4,102 wounded, and sustained another 11,155 deaths from disease. There were 16,978 casualties in the entire conflict with Mexico, and at Buena Vista, perhaps one of the most severe battles of the Mexican War, the Americans had 665 total casualties. The contrast between the Mexican War experience and the single day of Antietam was a very sobering one for the participants. To the casualty totals of Antietam one could add 1,813 Federals and 2,685 Confederates who fell at South Mountain, and 533 Federal and an undetermined number of Confederate casualties for the action at Crampton's Gap. The totals climb to 14,756 Federals and more than 16,409 Confederates, for a grand total in excess of 31,165 casualties for the Maryland Campaign. This was considered quite shocking, a general feeling reinforced by the circulation in civilian urban areas for the first time of photographs made on the battlefield of recent corpses. The horror of the war was brought home to many individuals, both civilian and military, by Antietam.

The engagements of Crampton's Gap, South Mountain, and Antietam represented strategic victory for the North. McClellan had successfully defended Washington, halted Lee's advance into Maryland, and had arguably inflicted a tactical defeat on the Army of Northern Virginia. Lee's army was, in any case, retreating into Virginia. From a Northern perspective, the negative aspect was that a great opportunity to destroy Robert E. Lee's Army of Northern Virginia completely had been missed. From a Southern viewpoint the Maryland operation contained some positive aspects, such as the reduction of Harper's Ferry along with capture of substantial Federal war material, and the removal, at least temporarily, of the armies from Virginia. The negative items were somewhat more ominous for the Confederacy. No large numbers of Marylanders had eagerly clamoured to join Southern ranks, nor were there many individuals in Kentucky of similar inclination. In addition, Lee's retreat from Sharpsburg, when coupled with Braxton Bragg's retreat in Kentucky following the battle of Perryville (8 October 1862), ended any realistic chance of European recognition of the Confederacy.

Robert E. Lee's decision to fight a battle at Antietam after the South Mountain operation is questionable. The Southern operational plan had been compromised when McClellan received a copy of Special Order 191, and Lee was fortunate that he was able to prevent the destruction of the Army of Northern Virginia in detail. Although McClellan's command style lessened the direct possibilities of disaster, it was still a considerable gamble for Lee to risk one of the Confederacy's principal armies on his reading of McClellan's character. Lee had done well enough with taking the war into Maryland after the Second Manassas Campaign and capturing Harper's Ferry. There may have been political reasons for risking a major engagement, but with its back to the Potomac River the Army of Northern Virginia faced the very real prospect of annihilation at Antietam. A more audacious Federal commander, with more attention to timing and command control than McClellan demonstrated, would have accomplished just that.

The counter argument may be that Lee knew his opponent, and that is certainly one of the marks of a great commander. Nevertheless, Robert E. Lee's fundamentally aggressive nature would cause the South further difficulties in Pennsylvania the following year during the Gettysburg Campaign and during subsequent operations in the autumn of 1863. The basic fact remains that Robert E. Lee fought a masterly defensive battle at Antietam with limited resources. He shifted his available reserves at the proper moment and gave everyone present throughout the day of 17 September the very clear impression that Robert E. Lee was in complete control of his army and of the battlefield. However, it was still very much, as Wellington remarked regard-ing Waterloo, a very near run thing, and final disaster was only averted by the fortuitous arrival of A. P. Hill's division from Harper's Ferry.

George McClellan has been severely criticized by his contemporaries and by historians for the slowness of his strategic movements and for his customary battlefield caution. McClellan's mission before 13 September was to keep the Army of the Potomac between Lee's army and Washington – his primary task was the defence of the Federal capital. The capture of Special Order 191 altered the situation considerably, and McClellan was presented with the chance to destroy Lee's formations one at a time if he moved swiftly. He ought to have ordered a night movement on the evening of 13 September, and as commander-in-chief he should have personally made certain that aggressive pursuit took place on the following day, after the engagements of South Mountain and Crampton's Gap had been fought. Not only was the pursuit dilatory, but Franklin's VI Corps was left slightly beyond Crampton's Gap virtually without orders until early on 17 September. McClellan wasted a further day, 16 September, in and around the Antietam position. He should have attacked directly with whatever forces were immediately at hand. If not all the Army of the Potomac was yet on the field, and even if his unit commanders were unfamiliar with the terrain, the same could be said of conditions prevalent at

◀ *After the battle, a Confederate surgeon, centre, shakes hands with a Federal counterpart near the Drunke Church, as both sides take care of the wounded.*

that moment in Lee's command. 'The mud', Napoleon remarked, 'is the same for everyone.' The opportunity was still available on 16 September to destroy elements of the Army of Northern Virginia, but McClellan failed to take advantage of it.

McClellan created a textbook tactical plan for the Antietam engagement. It was an operational conception that relied upon careful timing and close supervision. The uncoordinated nature of the assaults of I, XII and II Corps and the unconscionable delay in the advance of IX Corps have already been discussed – still, it very nearly worked. The Army of the Potomac fought extremely well between regimental and brigade level, but higher command control was lacking. The deficiency originated at the very top. McClellan remained on the eastern side of Antietam Creek through the majority of the battle, allowing his corps leaders to fight virtually their own separate engagements. He failed to supervise adequately the entirety of the Army of the Potomac. In the final analysis, however, it was the Confederate army that only escaped complete defeat by a narrow margin, and it was Lee's army that was retreating into Virginia by 19 September. McClellan had saved Washington and driven the invading rebels back south. That is one issue. The failure of the Army of the Potomac to destroy the Confederate Army of Northern Virginia totally is quite another. 'I feel that I have done all that can be asked', wrote McClellan to his wife on 20 September, 'in twice saving the country.'

The Battle of Antietam and Federal progress in halting the Confederate invasion of Kentucky that culminated at Perryville contributed in a dramatic fashion to altering the fundamental nature of the American Civil War. It became not only a conflict to preserve the Union but also a struggle to end the institution of Negro slavery in America. The destruction of the 'peculiar institution' had assumed the status of a moral crusade for many in the years before the War, although it is important to remember that in the nineteenth century it would not have been considered inconsistent to condemn the institution of slavery on moral grounds yet still have no interest in basic civil and social rights for the Black population as individuals. The Republican Party had argued for the elimination of slavery in Federal territories since 1856.

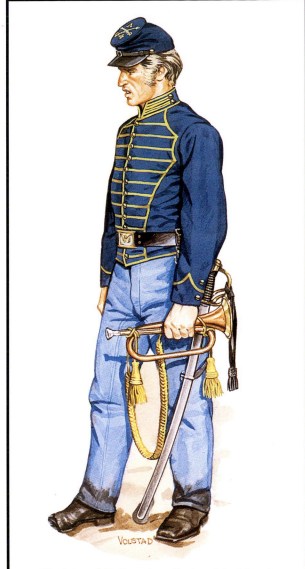

Musician, US Cavalry, distinguished by the braid on his chest, which would have been branch-of-service colour, as would the cord and tassels on the bugle. Painting by Ron Volstad.

The election of Abraham Lincoln in 1860 instigated the American Civil War. The course of the conflict would not only retain the Republic, but it would also ultimately destroy slavery. The Emancipation Proclamation issued soon after the battle of Antietam was not without precedent. The Lincoln administration declared slavery illegal in the territories on 19 June 1862. In the spring of 1862, Lincoln informed Congressmen of the loyal slave-owning border states that he was considering emancipation, and the 2nd Confiscation Act of July 1862 declared that all slaves taken as military contraband were to be considered free by Federal authorities. In addition, Lincoln informed his cabinet in July 1862 that he was considering a general emancipation statement. Secretary of State William Seward and others advised him to wait for Northern battlefield victories. Antietam encouraged Lincoln to make public the Emancipation Proclamation in a presidential decree of 22 September 1862, to take effect from 1 January 1863. It freed all slaves held in those parts of the nation in open rebellion, that is basically in the Confederacy. The immediate effect in terms of the numbers of Blacks freed may have been minimal, but it cannot be denied that the basic character of the American Civil War had been altered.

Antietam changed the military character of the war as well. The struggle seemed to have lost its innocence, for the staggering casualty lists and the savagery of a single day's fighting graphically illustrated that the war as an undertaking was a massive and serious concern. It would not be a conflict lightly pursued nor easily terminated. The American Civil War went beyond mere politics after Antietam. The War concerned itself with the maintenance of the Union, the destruction of Negro slavery, the survival of both Northern and Southern societies, and perhaps the alteration of the very fabric of the Republic. Antietam demonstrated to many participants that the events of which they were a part were not unimportant. Corporal Harrison Woodford of the 16th Connecticut, a veteran of Antietam, apparently thought so. He might stand for all the young men, living and dead, Northern and Southern, who fought in the Maryland Campaign in September 1862. Woodford wrote home to his sister on 26 September 1862, while his regiment was still encamped on the Antietam battlefield, asking her to remind his two younger brothers to assist their father in maintaining the family farm back in Connecticut. 'Tell them they must be good boys and help father all they can,' wrote Woodford. 'I have gone to fight for their freedom and for their interests in the future.'

◀ *General McClellan with President Lincoln at Antietam. Lee's manhandled men retired after the battle back to Virginia, where McClellan seemed content to let them remain. Lincoln wanted an immediate pursuit, but McClellan did little more than deploy pickets at the front. His patience finally exhausted, Lincoln relieved McClellan for the last time.*

THE BATTLEFIELD TODAY

The Antietam battlefield is located fourteen miles south of Hagerstown Maryland. It is best reached from Washington DC by proceeding north on interstate 270, heading towards Frederick, Maryland. The visitor, upon reaching Middletown, Maryland, should take Maryland alternate route 40, which will take him in approximately twelve miles to the South Mountain battlefield.

One can easily appreciate the defensive advantages enjoyed by Major General D. H. Hill's Division at South Mountain, and there are still visible remains of Confederate trenches. There are historical markers at the crest. The Federal positions are not marked at all, although a determined visitor could discover them with the aid of a geological survey map for the locality obtained at a number of government offices. Proceed next to Maryland on route 34 South. The Antietam battlefield, near Sharpsburg, is approximately five miles from South Mountain.

The Antietam battlefield is perhaps one of the best preserved fields of the American Civil War. It is extremely well marked, and national park service hard surfaced roads exist throughout the majority of the battlefield. The Antietam battlefield at this time has not been, fortunately, disgraced by the rampant commercialism that has surrounded and actually intruded upon the Gettysburg battlefield. The present day visitor can still appreciate the tactical problems faced by Civil War commanders at Antietam, and do so from the convenience of good modern roads that do not unduly affect the integrity of the field. In addition, the national park service museum and visitor centre is one of the best of its type in the United States. It contains an excellent museum, a splendid book store, and an orientation film that should really be the very first thing a visitor experiences. There is not, however, a restaurant worthy of that appellation in, or anywhere in reasonable driving distance of, Sharpsburg. The visitor should

carry his own rations, as driving to an eating establishment would drastically reduce time better spent observing the field. It is a small price to pay for keeping the field in a virtually pristine condition.

The visitor can obtain from the visitor centre an excellent map that very clearly explains a sensible route through the battlefield. It is not necessary to consider it here in detail, although a few observations are in order. The nature of the east woods very clearly explains the difficulties Major General Mansfield and his successors had in deploying Federal XII Corps. The exact spot where General Mansfield was mortally wounded is not well marked – it is to the north of the present marker.

The sunken road is perhaps the most striking spot on the battlefield, clearly demonstrating its value as a defensive position. I should recommend that after viewing the sunken road from the Confederate perspective, made easy by the modern road provided by the national park service, one should walk forward two hundred yards or so to the north, turn about and proceed back towards the sunken road. There is no more graphic display of the military importance of the position than coming upon the sunken road suddenly from the Federal perspective as Major General Sumner's II Corps soldiers did on 17 September 1862. It will take some physical effort on the part of the visitor to accomplish this, as the walking is not particularly easy, but he will be well rewarded by the result.

Burnside's Bridge must also be viewed from both the Confederate and Federal perspectives in order to be completely appreciated. One should start from the Federal side, cross the bridge, and walk up the rather steep slope. The visitor can then turn at the crest and view the bridge as the Confederate Georgia infantry saw it. It is clear how a small number of men could hold this position, and equally clear why it represented a rather daunting military problem to Burnside's Federal IX Corps. It should be pointed out that while Antietam Creek may not appear to be a significant military obstacle it is in fact rather deeper than it looks. In addition, a commander must consider not only the width of a water obstacle, but also the condition of the bank on the opposite shore. The bank held by the Confederates is very steep and presented a formidable obstacle to men advancing with equipment under fire.

General Burnside did have several brigades looking elsewhere for fording possibilities, but observation of the terrain in either direction from the stone bridge demonstrates the impossibility of moving artillery and large bodies of troops across Antietam Creek except at the bridge's location. The visitor cannot appreciate the tactical problem confronting General Burnside until he has viewed the terrain in the area.

A visit to the Antietam battlefield is perhaps one of the most enjoyable historical outings one could imagine. It clearly permits a more complete understanding of the battle, an understanding that can be accomplished with a minimum of physical difficulty. It is most certainly worth the time spent.

◀ *A detachment of the US Army's Signal Corps on Elk Ridge, which overlooked all Confederate positions and from where their troop movements could be seen and reported. The log tower was not actually built until after the battle, although the position was in use during the battle itself.*

CHRONOLOGY

29 September: The Battle of Second Manassas (also known as 2nd Bull Run), fought near Centreville, Virginia. The engagement concludes 30 September. The Federal Army of Virginia commanded by Major General John Pope is defeated by the Confederate Army of Northern Virginia commanded by General Robert E. Lee.

1 September: The Battle of Chantilly (also known as Ox Hill) fought by Federal forces under Major General Isaac Ingalls Stevens in an effort to cover the retirement of Major General Pope's army on Washington.

2 September: Major General George Brinton McClellan formally placed in command of the fortifications of Washington and all troops immediately concerned with the defence of the capital. McClellan's command consists of his own Army of the Potomac, the Army of Virginia and those forces in the defences of Washington.

4 September: The Army of Northern Virginia begins crossing the Potomac River into Maryland near Leesburg, Virginia. The operation completed 7 September.

5 September: The Army of Virginia and that of the Potomac are consolidated, Major General John Pope relieved from command of the Army of Virginia and ordered to Washington for further orders.

8 September: Major General Nathaniel Prentice Banks assumes command of the defences of Washington.

9 September: Lee, commanding the Army of Northern Virginia; issues Order 191 dividing the army into two wings: Major General Thomas Jonathan Jackson to advance on Harper's Ferry with six divisions, and Major General James Longstreet to advance on Hagerstown, Maryland with three divisions.

12 September: I, II, & III Corps/Army of Virginia redesignated XI, XII & I Corps/Army of the Potomac. The siege of Harper's Ferry, West Virginia, by Confederate forces commanded by Jackson begins.

13 September: McClellan receives Confederate Order 191 at Frederick, Maryland. By nightfall, Lee is informed that McClellan is in possession of Order 191 and orders an immediate withdrawal south of the Potomac.

14 September: BATTLE OF SOUTH MOUNTAIN (also known as Boonsborough, Boonsborough Gap or Turner's Gap). Major General Jesse Reno's IX Corps and Major General Joseph Hooker's I Corps clear Turner's Gap and Fox's Gap by 2200 after a stubborn defensive effort by the Confederate division commanded by Major General Daniel Harvey Hill. BATTLE OF CRAMPTON'S GAP also fought 14 September. Federal VI Corps commanded by Major General William Buel Franklin clears Crampton's Gap of Confederate forces by nightfall.

15 September: Confederate forces complete the capture of the Federal post at Harper's Ferry, West Virginia. Engagements fought on both Maryland & Bolivar Heights. Informed at Sharpsburg, Maryland, of Jackson's success at Harper's Ferry, Lee decides to concentrate his forces and offer battle along the Antietam Creek near Sharpsburg.

16 September: The Army of the Potomac arrives before the Confederate position along Antietam Creek. McClellan spends the remainder of the day in reconnaissance.

17 September: THE BATTLE OF ANTIETAM (also known as Sharpsburg). It must be pointed out that the exact timing of events at Antietam are, to some extent only approximate. There were a vast number of watches on the field, with no common standard. Dawn, which is listed for 17 September at 0543, Major General Hooker's Federal I Corps begins advance into the north woods with the divisions of Doubleday and Ricketts. The action against Jackson's Confederate divisions commanded by Lawton and D. R. Jones commences at approximately 0615.

0700: Brigadier General John Hood's Confederate Division counter-attacks Hooker's forces; bitter fighting in the cornfield and in the east woods.

0720: Hood's assault is repulsed; Federal XII Corps arrives on the field, deploying into the east woods by 0730.

0830: Major General Edwin Sumner brings Sedgwick's division of Federal II Corps into the east woods; severe fighting continues.

0900: Federal I and XII Corps are fought out by now; French's division of Federal II Corps arrives opposite the sunken road position, ultimately supported by Richardson's Division of II Corps. Fighting dies out on the Confederate left by 1030.

0930: Federal II Corps divisions of French and Richardson begin to assault the sunken road position in the Confederate centre held by Major General D. H. Hill's division. There is a great deal of bloody fighting until the position is finally taken by Federal forces at 1300, and then there is little subsequent activity at the Confederate centre.

Meanwhile in the south, Major General Ambrose Burnside has received several orders, at least from 1000, to assault the bridge to his front. The stone bridge is finally taken by elements of Sturgis's division of Federal IX Corps at 1300. The remainder of the Federal IX Corps is across Antietam Creek and advancing towards Sharpsburg by 1500.

Between 1545 and 1600, the Confederate division commanded by Major General Ambrose Powell Hill begins arriving on the field, after completing a seventeen mile march from the Harper's Ferry area. Hill's division counter-attacks Federal IX Corps, the action completed by 1630.

There is no further activity of significance anywhere on the field.

18 September: The Army of Northern Virginia begins recrossing the Potomac River into Virginia near Shepherdstown, West Virginia. The operation is completed on 19 September.

22 September: President Abraham Lincoln issues the Emancipation Proclamation, to take effect 1 January 1863.

7 November: Major General McClellan relieved from command of the Army of the Potomac and ordered to New Jersey to await further orders. Major General Ambrose Burnside assigned to the command of the Army of the Potomac.

A GUIDE TO FURTHER READING

The Maryland Campaign of 1862 is perhaps one of the most thoroughly documented military operations of the American Civil War. The printed sources are numerous and easily available. The starting point for any serious research must be *The War of the Rebellion, A Compilation of the Official Records of the Union and Confederate Armies*, Series I, Volume XIX, Parts 1 & 2, (Washington DC: the Government Printing Office, 1887). These are the volumes concerning the 1862 Maryland Campaign. The Official Records, or simply the 'ORs' as most insiders call them, contain reports filed by both Federal and Confederate unit commanders from army level through brigade, and frequently for regimental and independent batteries. Officers were required to submit reports to their immediate superiors at regular intervals. These reports were collected by the United States War Department and published in well over one hundred volumes during the second half of the nineteenth century. The Official Records represent a dynamic and extraordinarily complete account of military operations from the perspective of the officers concerned with their direction. One must bear in mind, however, that these individuals were conscious they were writing for the edification of posterity. In addition, it was not uncommon for officers to submit reports months after the conclusion of the events they described. The Official Records remain, none the less, the single most important source for the study of any military operation of the American Civil War. The 'ORs' are available in most American University libraries in their original state, and the entire set has been recently reprinted.

A number of articles written after the conclusion of the War by various Federal and Confederate military commanders for *Century Magazine*, were collected in the *Battles and Leaders* series. The volume concerning the 1862 Maryland Campaign is, *North to Antietam, Battles and Leaders of the Civil War*, (New York, New York: Thomas Yoseloff Press Inc. 1956). The articles are interesting because the authors have had time for reflection since the termination of the War, although one should remember that these pieces were written when post-war controversies were very much alive. The series is available in a reprinted edition.

A study of the Maryland Campaign should not ignore General McClellan's description of events contained in, *McClellan's Own Story, The War for the Union*, (New York, New York: Charles L. Webster & Co. Inc. 1887). One must also consult *The Civil War Papers of George B. McClellan, Selected Correspondence 1860 to 1865*, edited by Stephen W. Sears, (New York, New York: Ticknor & Fields Publishing Co. Inc. 1989.) General Lee did not construct a post-war memoir, although he was collecting material for such an endeavour before he died in 1870. Douglas Southall Freeman does provide a clear perspective of Lee's command style in *Lee's Lieutenants, A Study in Command*, Volume II 'Cedar Mountain to Chancellorsville', (New York, New York: Charles Scribner's Sons, 1942, reprinted 1972).

The absolute best single-volume secondary source on the Antietam Campaign remains James V. Murfin's, *The Gleam of Bayonets, the Antietam Campaign and the Maryland Campaign of 1862* (New York and London: Thomas Yoseloff 1965). Stephen W. Sears has provided an adequate addition to Murfin with his *Landscape Turned Red, the Battle of Antietam*, (New York, New York: Ticknor & Fields Publishing Co. Inc. 1983). John M. Priest has added to the literature with a collection of individual soldier's recollections, *Antietam, The Soldier's Battle*, (Shippensburg, Pennsylvania: White Mane Publishing Co. Inc. 1989). Colonel Jennings Cropper Wise's *The Long Arm of Lee, A History of the Artillery of the Army of Northern Virginia*, Volume I, (Richmond, Virginia: Owens Publishing

Co. Inc. 1915, reprinted 1988), provides interesting commentary on Southern artillery operations during the Maryland Campaign.

Jay Luvas & Harold W. Nelson make a tour of the battle areas easy with, *The United States Army War College Guide to the Battle of Antietam and the Maryland Campaign of 1862*. It demonstrates the accessibility, or lack of accessibility to the relevant sites, along with an adequate historical commentary of events as they developed. Finally, William A. Frassanito considers the relationship of photography and nineteenth century warfare, employing the Antietam Campaign as a case study in his, *Antietam, The Photographic Legacy of America's Bloodiest Day*, (New York, New York: Charles Scribner's Sons, 1978).

INDEX

Figures in **bold** refer to illustrations

Antietam Creek 44, **45**, 73, 90
Army of North Virginia 7, 9, 17, 25, 85-86
  Anderson' Division 61, 64, 69
    Mahone's Brigade 33-34, 35
  A. P. Hill's Division 80-81, 84
  D. H. Hill's Division 40, 55, 60-61
    at Turner's Gap 35-36, 37
  Hood's Division 47, 48-49
  Jackson's Division 45-47, 55-56
  Jones's Division
    Toombs's Brigade 76-77
  McLaw's Division 56-59
  order of battle 30-32
  surgeon **71**
  Walker's Division 56-59
Army of the Potomac 7, 7-8, 12, 25, 87
  I (Hooker's) Corps 33, **44**, 45, **45**,45-47, 53
    Meade's Division 39-40
    'Iron Brigade' 40, 48-49
    'Pennsylvania Reserves' 39-40
  II (Sumner's) Corps 53-56, 59
    French's Division 60, 62-64, **63**
    'Irish Brigade' 63-64, **75**
    Sedgwick's Division 57-59
  VI (Franklin's) Corps 33-35, 41, 59
  IX (Burnside's) Corps 33, 36-37, 40, 56, 81
    9th New York, Hawkin's Zouaves **5**, **82**
    crosses Antietam Creek 75-80
    Kanawha Division 36-37, 81, 84
  XII (Mansfield's) Corps 45, 49, 52-53, **52-53**
  casualties 85
  confidence in McClellan 8-9, 15-16
  order of battle 26-30
  signal corps **90**
  uniforms
    cavalry **22**, **87**

infantry **27**, **46**, **59**, **75**
Army of the United States (1860) 21
Army of Virginia 7, 8-9
artillery 21, 23, **24**, **36**

Bartlett, Colonel Joseph Jackson, 27th New York Volunteers (1834-93) 34-35
Bloody Lane 60-71, **66-67**(map)
Burnside, Major General Ambrose Everett (1824-81) 17, **17**, 28, 43-44, 73, 75
  orders from McClellan 73, 76
  at Turner's Gap 35, 37
Burnside Bridge **72**, **73**, **84**, **89-90**
  assault on **23**, 72-84, **74**, **76**, **77**, **78-79**(map)

casualties 59, 85, 96
  at Crampton's Gap 35
cavalry 23, 24
Chantilly, Battle of, 1 September 1862 7, **7**
chronology 91-92
Confederate Conscription Act (1862) 25
cornfield, the 46, **46-47**, 48-49
Cox, Brigadier General Jacob Dolson (1828-1900) 36-37, 44
Crompton's Gap, Battle of, 14 September 1862 13, 33-35, **34**(map)

discipline 22
dispositions 45, **50-51**(map), **83**(map)
Dunkard Church 45, **48**, 55, **69**, **86**

East Woods 45, 46, 52-53, 89
Elk Ridge **90**

formations 23
Fox's Gap 35-37, **38**(map)
Franklin, Major General William (1823-1903), 33, **35**, 59

Garland, Brigadier Samuel (1830-62) 35-36, 37
Gorman, Brigadier General Willis Arnold (1816-76) 56, 58-59
Greene, Brigadier General George Sears (1801-99), 52

Harper's Ferry 11, **13**, 35, 41, 42, 80
Hays, Lieutenant Colonel Rutherford Birchard (1822-93) 36-37
Hill, Major General Ambrose Powell (1825-65) **10**, 20, **20**, 80-81
Hill, Major General Daniel Harvey (1821-89) 11, 20, 35, 37, **43**, **61**
Hood, Brigadier General John Bell (1831-79) 20, **49**
Hooker, Major General Joseph (1814-79) 16-17, **16**, 46, 49
'Hooker's Division' 16-17

Jackson, Major General Thomas Jonathan 'Stonewall' (1824-63) 11, 19-20, **19**, 47
Jacob Grove house **42**

Kearny, Major General Philip (1814-62) **7**
Kimball, Brigadier General Nathan (1823-98) 62-63, 65

Lee, General Robert Edward (1807-70) 9, **10**, **18**, 47, 85-86
  background 17-19
  battle plan 42-43
  criticism of 42
  views on McClellan 15
Lincoln, Abraham, President USA (1809-65) 7, 8, 87-88, **88**
Longstreet, Major General James (1821-1904) 11, **19**
Loudoun Heights **13**

Manassas, Second Battle of, 29 August 1862 7, 8
Mansfield, Major General Joseph

King Fenno (1803-62) 49, **49**, 52-53

Maryland **6**(map), 9-11, 43, 85

McClellan, Major General George Brinton (1826-85) **2**, 8-9, **12**, 33, **58**, **88**
achievement 85
background 15-16
battle plan 43-44, 72
caution of 3, 9, 43, 86-87, 95
orders to Burnside 72-73

McLaws, Major General Lafayette (1821-97) 56-57, **58**

Meade, Brigadier General George Gordon (1815-72) 39, **48**

Meagher, Brigadier General Thomas Francis (1823-67) 63-64

Mexican War (1846-7) 15, 16, 17, 19, 20, 85

Miles, Lieutenant Colonel Nelson A, 61st New York Infantry Regiment **71**

Mumma house **68**

Munford, Colonel Thomas Taylor (1831-?), 2nd Virginia Cavalry 33-34

officers 21-22

organisation 23

Pleasonton, Brigadier General Alfred (1824-97) 24

Pope, Major General John (1822-92) 7-8, 9

Porter, Major General Fitz-John (1822-1901) **84**

Potomac River **8**, 9, 42

Powell, Captain William H, 4th United States Infantry Regiment, V Corps 8-9

propaganda, Northern **20-21**

Pry House **57**

raiding 24

Reno, Major General Jesse Lee (1823-62) 28, 33, 40, **41**

Richardson, Major General Israel Bush (1815-62) **70**

Rodes, Brigadier General Robert Emmet (1829-64) 40, 64-65

Rodman, Brigadier General Isaac Peace (1822-62) **81**

Roulette House **63**

Sedgwick, Major General John (1813-64) **54**

Sharpsburg 80, 81

Slocum, Major General Henry Warner (1827-94) 34

South Mountain 12, 13, **14**(map), 28, 33-41, 89

Special Order 191 11-13, 11(text), 33, 41, 42, 85

straggling 25

Stevens, Major General Isaac Ingalls (1818-62) 7, 22

Sturgis, Brigadier General Samuel Davis (1822-89) 77

Sumner, Major General Edwin Vose (1797-1863) 54-55, **55**, 59

sunken road 60-61, **60-61**, **64**, **65**, **70**, 89
assault on 62-64, 65, 68, 70

Toombs, Brigadier General Robert Augustus (1810-85) 76

training 22

troops 21-22

Turner's Gap, Battle of, 14 September 1862 13, **33**, 35-41, **38**(map), **39**(map)

United States Military Academy (West Point) 15, 16, 17, 19, 20, 22, 39, 57

Walker, Major General John G (1822-93) **13**

wargaming 95-96

Washington Garrison 29-30

weapons 23-24

West Woods 55, 57-59

western theatre of operations 10

Williams, Brigadier General Alpheus Starkey (1810-78) 53

Woodford, Corporal Harrison, I Company/16th Connecticut Volunteers 9, 17, 35, 88